SKISPOTS

LES DE

...nston

Original concept by **Francis Johnston**
Original photography by the author, unless otherwise credited
Front cover photography courtesy of Salomon Sports, www.salomonsports.com

Produced by the Bridgewater Book Company
Project Editor: Emily Casey Bailey
Project Designer: Lisa McCormick

Published by Thomas Cook Publishing
PO Box 227, The Thomas Cook Business Park, Unit 15/16, Coningsby Road,
Peterborough PE3 8SB, United Kingdom
email: books@thomascook.com
www.thomascookpublishing.com
+44 (0) 1733 416477

ISBN-13: 978-1-84157-514-8
ISBN-10: 1-84157-514-3
Head of Thomas Cook Publishing: Chris Young
Project Editor: Kelly Anne Pipes
Production/DTP: Steven Collins

ACKNOWLEDGEMENTS

This book is dedicated to Sofia Barbas and all my family. It is the result of many wonderful days and nights in the mountains, aided by and accompanied by some great characters. Specific thanks go to Héléna Hospital and Jeanne Mounaut at the Office du Tourisme de Les Deux Alpes; Didier Grier and Niels Martin at the Office du Tourisme de La Meije; Stephan Corporon at the Comité Départemental du Tourisme de l'Isère; Mike Stoker at Salomon Sports; Jennifer Thyer for initial insights; and to Sofia for research assistance and for compiling the Language section.

CONTENTS

SYMBOLS KEY

The following is a key to the symbols used throughout this book:

- bucket lift
- cable car
- gondola lift
- chair lift
- declutchable chair lift
- button lift
- magic carpet
- rope tow
- funicular railway
- warning – difficult lift
- two-way lift
- cross-country ski circuit
- base station
- equipment rental
- tool point
- ski pass sales point
- elevator
- information office
- parking
- bus stop
- WC
- piste difficulty rating
- ATM cash machine
- telephone
- post office
- church
- supermarket
- restaurant
- café
- bar
- medical point
- pharmacy

---

t telephone · f fax · e email · w website address

a address · opening times · ! important · ➔ page reference

€ budget price · €€ mid-range price · €€€ most expensive

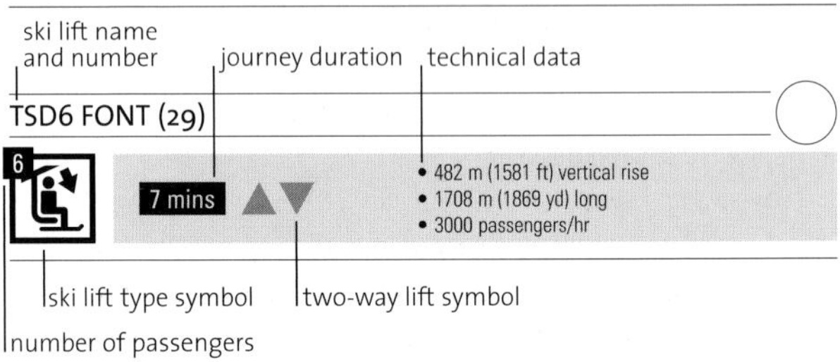

---

ski lift name and number · journey duration · technical data

TSD6 FONT (29)

6 · 7 mins · ▲▼

- 482 m (1581 ft) vertical rise
- 1708 m (1869 yd) long
- 3000 passengers/hr

ski lift type symbol · two-way lift symbol

number of passengers

INTRODUCTION TO SKISPOTS

Welcome to SkiSpots, an innovative series of specialist guidebooks to Europe's top ski regions, designed and compiled by some of Europe's most experienced snowsports professionals. Whether you ski, board, blade or Langlauf, are a piste virgin or a seasoned powder hound, SkiSpots are as indispensable as your ski pass.

With a snowsports-centric layout and a snowsports-specific information flow, these guides are focused on the major linked ski domains and the resorts that access them: with historical snowfall charts and analysis as a guide to the best dates to visit for optimum snow conditions; base station layouts and resort street plans; detailed information and critiques on all principal ski lifts and pistes; ideas for alternative activities and après ski; and complemented by the history, culture, gastronomy, language and attractions of the surrounding region.

Action-packed and filled with insider intelligence and technical expertise, with a wealth of general information to keep non-skiers interested too, SkiSpots are the next best thing to having a private mountain guide.

On a piste map, the sun is always shining, the snow is always powder perfect, the visibility is always excellent and the links are always open. SkiSpots provide an invaluable extension to your piste map, describing the ski area in three dimensions, clarifying ambiguous and complicated routes, directing you away from the links that don't work and towards the areas that will deliver the most satisfying descents.

The author has visited every corner of the resorts and ski domains, taken and timed every lift, skied every piste and most of the powder fields in between and visited every recommended bar and restaurant – it's a dirty job, but someone's got to do it!

Snow excites a childlike fascination in us all; who hasn't felt the urge to rush out and throw a snowball after even the slightest frosting of this magical powder on a crisp winter morning? The first priority of this guidebook is to stimulate your excitement about the mountains, striving to inform and nourish your enjoyment of this wonderful environment and direct you to the best that the resorts and ski areas have to offer.

The first part of the book gives you a flavour of the region you are visiting, detailing the history of the area and the pioneering beginnings of the extensive snowsports infrastructure that you enjoy today; with an overview on the regional food and drink and a basic snowsports-centric vocabulary in the local language to help you engage more readily with your hosts and speed up assistance if and when you require it.

The second part of the guide begins with an all-important briefing on the dangers of the mountains in winter, and the tried-and-tested ways of minimizing the risks to which you expose yourself when participating in adventure sports in this environment; together with the rules and regulations that all slope users have to observe. Next comes the introduction to each major resort and ski area and how to access them; with street plans, piste maps and ski area data; ski pass information, resort transport, equipment hire, ski schools, childcare, resort and ski area services; plus snowfall history charts. Each sector of the ski area is then broken down by base station layout, first access points and onward links, with a detailed lift-by-lift description and piste-by-piste critique; every mountain bar and restaurant is covered in depth and suggested point-to-point itineraries are illustrated to assist with route planning to help you squeeze the maximum potential out of your day.

When the après-ski begins, SkiSpots continue with you by suggesting alternative activities and listing the cafés, restaurants, bars and clubs in which to round off your day. The book finishes with some ideas for days away from the pistes, together with an insight into the attractions of the region in summer.

www.ski-ride.com

Due to the ephemeral nature of snow, and the dynamic nature of the mountain environment and the snowsports industry, resort facilities and ski area boundaries can change. Therefore the SkiSpots series is also supported by an Internet portal, delivering up-to-the-minute news and links to the ski areas: on-site webcams, live snow reports and current weather information, resort fact sheets, events diary, tour operator links and much more, enhancing both this guidebook and your trip.

HOW TO USE THIS BOOK

SkiSpots travel guides give ski lift and piste information in a unique graphical format. Detailed information is given on the type of ski lift, journey duration, capacity, directions to follow on arrival and onward links. All principal pistes are covered and are colour-coded by level of difficulty with detailed access routes, descriptions of terrain, best lines of descent and onward links, accompanied by regular piste map illustrations to help you in real-time itinerary planning and route-finding on-the-move.

Point-to-point route-finder information is not necessarily the quickest option, but rather the best on-piste direction to deliver the most enjoyable route between the specified points. The route-finders are detailed for both competent novices and good intermediates.

ABOUT THE AUTHOR

Francis (Gary) Johnston was born in County Down, Northern Ireland. He was previously employed at a senior level with two of the UK's leading Ski, Lakes & Mountains tour operators, having lived and worked in Andorra, Spain and Portugal. He has also worked in or visited most of the leading French, Austrian and Italian ski resorts, having personally accompanied and guided well over four thousand visitors and travel industry professionals during that time.

Francis now divides his time between Andorra, France and Brighton in England, travelling up to six months each year in the Alps and Pyrenees.

! The Alpine environment can be harsh and dangerous, but it is also very fragile – please respect it and leave nothing but your tracks in the snow.

REGIONAL INTRODUCTION

Isère & Oisans

WELCOME – BIENVENUE

Les Deux Alpes lies in the Oisans area of France's Isère *département*; a land of diverse physical contrasts which straddles the boundary between the Northern and Southern Alps. Over 60 distinct types of landscape have been classified in Isère – the greatest number for any area in France, ranging from sun-drenched arable plains and fertile river valleys to sheer escarpments and deep caverns; rolling wooded hills and lush high-altitude meadows to Alpine peaks and glacial deserts. This land also has a rich human landscape, filled with history and tradition; a land where respect and enthusiasm for local customs and culture are protected and encouraged, preserving much of the original charm of the region and adding to its already strong appeal as a world-class mountain-holiday destination.

Isère's capital Grenoble is an Olympic city and regarded as the capital of the French Alps; along with Innsbruck in Austria it is one of the most populous and important cities in this backbone of Europe. Stendal (pseudonym of Henri Beyle, 1783–1842, author of *Le Rouge et le Noir*) was a native of the city and described it as having 'a mountain at the end of every street'; despite its lofty surroundings, the city paradoxically also has the distinction of being France's flattest city, spread out at the wide confluence point of the Isère and Drac rivers. It houses one of Europe's oldest universities and has one of France's largest student/resident ratios, infusing the city with a young and vibrant atmosphere. In contrast to its long and illustrious past, the city and its environs are now a thrusting technological heartland, often referred to as the 'Silicon Valley of France'.

Grenoble: 'a mountain at the end of every street'

SNOWSPORTS PEDIGREE

Isère's ski stations jockey for position in snowsports' premier league: Chamrousse in the Chaine de Belledonne, just outside Grenoble, hosted the 1968 Winter Games; the Vercors Massif is a mecca for Nordic ski enthusiasts, boasting over 800 km (500 miles) of cross-county trails; and the towering glacial massifs of the Grandes Rousses and Ecrins, south-east of Grenoble, are home to Les Deux Alpes and Alpe d'Huez – the former, focused around Europe's largest skiable glacier and the latter, one of Europe's largest linked ski domains.

Despite their southern latitude, these resorts are also at high enough altitudes to guarantee a long ski season and are blessed with favourable microclimates that ensure sufficiently regular snowfalls. The influence of the south is still felt though in the stability of the local weather patterns and, when not snowing, the skies above the slopes are often bluebird clear and provide first-rate visibility.

The extent of the ski areas means that there is something here for everyone, from nervous novices to experienced adrenaline junkies, and the Oisans resorts are some of France's, and therefore the world's, best all-round snowsports destinations.

REGIONAL STATISTICS

- 36 ski stations, 13 of which are 'internationally classified'
- 20 resorts specializing in Nordic skiing
- A total of 445 ski lifts across the region's resorts
- More than 2500 km (1563 miles) of pistes
- Further info: www.isere-tourisme.com and www.oisans.com

HISTORY & CULTURE
Regional development

REGIONAL IDENTITY

The Celtic and Gallic tribes that founded the earliest settled communities in these high and harsh Alpine valleys included the Vocontii and the fierce Allobroges, who fought alongside Vercingétorix the Gaul, but from 121 BC onwards they gradually succumbed to the might of the Roman Empire. Burgundian tribes from the Rhine that were compliant to Rome were allowed to settle in their place, around present-day Grenoble and Chambéry, and the area began to develop as a defined region. After the fall of the Roman Empire, the territory became part of the Kingdom of Burgundy and was subject to frequent changes of fortune following various conflicts during the next five centuries. Burgundy was eventually incorporated into the Holy Roman Empire in 1032 and the vast kingdom was split into feudal superstates, corresponding more or less with present-day Savoie, Provence and Isère.

To the north, Savoie rose to become one of the most politically powerful states in Europe, ruling over the key Alpine passes and much of north-west Italy; to the south, Provence was controlled by the commercially astute Catalan Counts of Forcalquier, Toulouse and Barcelona; whilst the large, strategically important, buffer state between these two dynamic neighbours came under the dominion of the Counts of Albon. It is this latter extensive territory that corresponds with present-day Isère.

THE DAUPHINÉ

One of the most influential of the Albons, Guigues IV, had Dauphin as his second name and his county became known as the Dauphiné in his honour, with each successive ruler adopting the title of Dauphin; the Isère region is still recognized by this ancient sobriquet to the present day.

In the 14th century, the Dauphin Humbert II founded Grenoble university; he was an extravagant patron of the arts and benefactor of the church, spending lavish amounts on grandiose cultural projects. His participation in the crusades to the Holy Land drained his already dwindling state coffers to such an extent that upon his return in 1349 he abdicated and sold the Dauphiné to Philippe VI of Valois, King of France; the title of Dauphin was then conferred on the heir to the French throne.

THE FRENCH REVOLUTION

In 1447, the Dauphin Louis II (the future King Louis XI) established his court in the Dauphiné, abolished the feudal system and established the Parliament of Grenoble. Unfortunately this early example of local government didn't find favour with future kings and many political institutions were forcibly re-centralized back to the French crown. This erosion of democracy caused nation-wide civil discontent, which became focused by events developing in the Dauphiné: on 21 July 1788, the États du Dauphiné (the regional assembly) met at the Château de Vizille south-east of Grenoble. After a marathon full-day meeting, the assembly ratified a resolution which registered disapproval at the king's meddling in politics and his suppression of Parliament; it demanded a conference of all of the nation's regional assemblies and recognition of individual freedom for all French citizens. The assembly's resolution matched the national zeitgeist and unrest came to a head a year later after the king proscribed the regional assemblies altogether and attempted to ban the recently self-declared National Assembly. The inhabitants of most French cities rebelled; in Paris the Bastille was stormed and the whole nation rose against the monarchy and aristocracy.

Isère is thus regarded as the cradle of the French Revolution and the Château de Vizille (see page 217) today houses France's only specialized museum dedicated to this pivotal period of French history.

In 1791, the aristocratic provinces were broken up and the Dauphiné was divided up into three départements: Isère, Drôme and Hautes-Alpes.

ROUTE NAPOLEON

Napoleon I, on his return from exile on Elba in 1815, crossed the Southern Alps with a small army of supporters and passed into Isère via Corps and La Mure. At Laffrey, just 6 km (3¾ miles) south of Vizille, he encountered the troops of Louis XVIII at the historic 'meeting of the praire', where he famously won the hearts and minds of his would-be opposition by walking straight up to them and baring his chest, inviting them to shot him there and then if they truly didn't believe in his right to lead them as Emperor again. In recognition of Napoleon's past military glories in the expansion of the French Empire, the royal troops switched allegiance and marched side-by-side with him towards Grenoble. Present-day travellers in this region can follow the way-marked route of his eventually triumphant return, known as The Route Napoleon.

TOWARDS THE PRESENT DAY

In the mid-19th century, research by Louis Vicat (1786–1861) into Roman construction technology lead to the rediscovery of the process of cement production. The extensive calcareous deposits in the valleys around Grenoble proved to be an ideal raw material for the process, prompting an industrial boom for the region and driving the expansion of Grenoble into the Romanche valley.

Dauphiné cement became a major export earner and many of New York's earliest skyscrapers were constructed using it. Coal mining and paper milling were the other two big primary industries fuelling the prosperity of the region as a whole, whilst slate quarrying in the Vénéon valley contributed specifically to the economic wealth of the Oisans area and remained an important industry there right up to the outbreak of World War II.

During the war, the Resistance were particularly active throughout Isère, with Grenoble regarded as the 'capital of the maquis'. The reprisals and general destruction of the Nazi occupation had a terrible effect on the region however, and it was left weakened both demographically and economically.

Following the war, many fertile Alpine foothills and river valleys were established as agricultural areas, specializing in dairy products and fruit cultivation, but the most dramatic reversal of fortunes resulted from the rapid development of hydroelectricity, fuelling the advancement of related industries such as electrometallurgy and electrochemistry in the valleys around Grenoble. The historic university of Grenoble became an important centre of study for these technologies, as well as nuclear science, and the campus is still regarded today as one the most important research and development centres in Europe.

The steady growth of the mountain tourist industry also contributed to Isère's return to the world stage: the first tourist office in France was created in Grenoble, the surrounding mountains of the Chaine de Belledonne and Grandes Rousses and the Glaciers du Monts-de-Lans were developed as international ski stations and in 1968 the city hosted the Winter Olympics, centred on the Belledonne resort of Chamrousse, with the bobsleigh event held at Alpe d'Huez.

MONT-DE-LANS & VENOSC

The Romanche valley has always been an important trans-Alpine trade route; sections of a Roman road can be seen at Bons near Mont-de-Lans. The earliest inhabitants of Mont-de-Lans and Venosc survived by keeping dairy animals on the high meadows (the 'alpes') in summer, hawking their produce to passing travellers and working as peddlers in winter. Dwellings and barns were established on the upper pastures, but were deserted during the long winters when the inhabitants returned to the slightly more sheltered lower villages.

The better opportunities and easier life of the more modern and prosperous lowland towns and cities drew most of the younger inhabitants away. Then, in the early 1900s, a remarkable reversal of fortunes changed the dynamics of these Alpine regions: the newly fashionable sport of skiing altered perceptions of the once negative climatic conditions and suddenly became one of the area's most valuable assets.

SKI HISTORY

In the 1930s, development began on a winter sports resort on the Alpe de Mont-de-Lans and Alpe de Venosc, but the first attempts failed when the only drag lift collapsed. The true birth of the resort was in 1946 when a button lift was built on the Pied Moutet slopes and the new village was named Les Deux Alpes. From this rudimentary beginning, the resort gradually expanded, and when the last engineering obstacles were overcome to reach the summit of the Dôme de la Lauze in 1984, the resort became one of the top ten ski resorts in France for the sheer extent of its ski area. Les Deux Alpes, has now become a major international resort and an important contributor to the regional economy.

FOOD & DRINK

Gastronomy

TRADITIONAL MOUNTAIN FARE

Regional gastronomy has too often been regarded as of secondary importance in the snowsports holiday experience. Now, however, more travellers are seeking to complement their time in the mountains with great meals too. The rich diversity of European regional cuisine is nowhere more enjoyable than in the actual regions that created it.

Produce of Isère and Savoie

France consistently lives up to its reputation as the world's foremost provider of gourmet food and fine wine, and you could read a whole library of books on French gastronomy alone. The produce and specialities of Isère have a history and tradition intertwined with those of neighbouring Savoie; narrowing the focus to the specialities of these two départements should give you a flavour of the rich tradition of wholesome mountain cooking that is alive and well in these important Alpine regions.

With very little mountain land area suitable for intensive farming, surviving the harsh high altitude winters through history required a rustic, hearty diet which made full use of the limited range of indigenous foodstuffs. Isère mountain cuisine was therefore born out of necessity, relying heavily on dairy products from cows, goats and sheep; meat; game; a few hardy fruit and vegetable crops; together with cured and dried foodstuffs harvested and preserved during the summer and autumn.

REGIONAL PRODUCE

chou: Savoy cabbage; probably the most internationally renowned vegetable from the French Alps and a real staple of the local diet

coings: quinces; acidic pear-shaped fruit. These are popular mountain fruits because they are quite hardy and flourish where softer fruit would struggle. An important source of vitamin C in a mountain diet and used to make preserves and desserts such as rissoles – quince paste spread on cornmeal fingers and then baked or deep-fried and served warm sprinkled with sugar

poires: pears; Conference, Williams and Général Leclerc are the three most common and easily recognized varieties of the half-a-dozen regional favourites. The fresh Savoie fruit and juice carries an *Indication Géographique Protégée* (IGP) label protected by EU law and guaranteeing provenance from particular regions

pommes: apples; Golden Delicious, Jonagold, Elstar, Melrose and Idared are the most common among the dozen or so preferred varieties grown in this and the neighbouring Savoie region

pommes de terre: potatoes; a staple of the Isère diet ever since they were introduced into the Dauphiné province from the neighbouring Duchy of Savoie, long before either were part of France

noix de Grenoble: walnuts of Grenoble. Nuts form an important part of the high altitude mountain diet, being easy to store, long keeping, and packed with energy. They are used in everything: bread, starters, main courses and desserts. Walnut by-products are numerous and include walnut oil, jam and confectionery. Walnuts have been an emblematic product of Isère since the eleventh and Grenoble walnuts were awarded an *Appellation d'Origine Contrôlée* (AOC) (see page 25) in 1938. The principal areas of cultivation are located along the Isère valley west of Grenoble, particularly around Vinay and in the Sud-Grésivaudan region.

'Tomme' cheese from Savoie

DAIRY PRODUCTS

Dairy herds play a major part in the gastronomic heritage of the Isère and Savoie, and their produce brims with the flavour and goodness of this pure environment. Alpine-specific breeds of cattle, mostly Abondance and Tarine, are pastured on the high-altitude meadows during the short Alpine summer from mid-June to early September. The meadows are watered by the glacial runoffs. Individual farm herds are usually quite small, but in late spring are combined with the cattle from neighbouring farms for the transhumance (transfer) up to the meadows as soon as the snows have cleared.

Chevrotin goats have also been farmed in these regions for many centuries and the Savoie Chevrotin cheese carries an AOC. Like the cattle, the goats are subject to a transhumance every spring to the high-altitude meadows, though the goats range much further and higher. Milking takes place two times each day and the cheese-making process is still mainly carried out by hand on-site in high-altitude barns.

CHEESES

Saint-Marcellin: this is, by tradition, a goat's milk cheese, but nowadays it is made using a milder blend of goat's and cow's milk. The first historic mention of Saint-Marcellin cheese dates from the 15th: on the occasion of a hunt, the Dauphin Louis II, the future King Louis XI, was injured and was looked after by local

QUALITY GUARANTEES

Indication Géographique Protégée (IGP): established by the European Commission to protect geographic names applied to agricultural products, such as Savoie apples and pears

Label Régional Savoie: a guarantee of provenance from the Savoie region and, by association, a guarantee of quality

Appellation d'Origine Contrôlée (AOC): official provenance and quality guarantee protected by European Commission law. AOC recognizes and protects the specific characteristics inherent in regional produce as a subtle and unreproducable blend of geographic position, reputation, tradition and knowledge passed down from generation to generation, producing a unique set of circumstances which impart a peculiar quality to the product. Corresponds to the Europe-wide *Appellation d'Origine Protégée* (AOP), protected designation of origin law. A guarantee of provenance from a particular region and, by association, a guarantee of production quality, rigorous selection process and traceability.

woodcutters, who gave him some cheese to eat. Louis proclaimed it delicious and Saint-Marcellin became a regular feature on the table of the French king

Bleu de Vercors-Sassenage: AOC; a medium-strength creamy blue cheese produced since the Middle Ages by the farmers of the Vercors, originally as a tax paid to the Lord of Sassenage. It is often used in *fondue savoyarde*

Tomme de Belledonne: in the regional dialects, the word Tomme simply means 'cheese', but also refers to the mould in which the cheeses are pressed. A medium-hard cheese with small holes and a rich creamy taste. It is now promoted as an organic product (*agriculture biologique*)

Isère dairy favourites

Reblochon AOC: strong-smelling soft cheese made with milk from Abondance cattle, which is pressed into hand-sized rounds. One of the prime ingredients of *tartiflette* (see page 31), this cheese is made traditionally from the sweeter second milking (the *rebloche*) and has a recorded history dating back to the 13th century

Beaufort AOC: known as the 'Prince of Gruyères', this is a strong hard cheese moulded into large rounds using beechwood hoops, which not only maintain the shape but also give the cheese its distinctive concave edge. Beaufort has a delicate ivory colour but the flavour is strong. Used in *fondue savoyarde* and in gratin dishes, but equally well-suited to simple presentation in a cheeseboard selection

Emmental de Savoie: cow's milk cheese with a rich, creamy interior and smooth with well-distributed holes. Traditionally ripened for 75 days and awarded a Savoie label

Chevrotin AOC: goat's milk cheese mostly from the Aravis area of Haute Savoie, around the ski resort of La Clusaz. Produced exclusively on individual farms, not collectives

Tamié: a fine cow's milk cheese produced by Trappist monks near Albertville; its packaging is instantly recognizable as it bears the Maltese cross

CURED MEATS & SAUSAGES

Ham (*jambon*) and cured sausages (*salaisons*) are staples of the Alpine diet, as they are an excellent way to preserve meat for the long winters. The most typical regional ham is the mildly salted *jambon de Savoie* , a dry-cured mountain ham similar to Parma ham, which is aged for at least 9–12 months and served in wafer-thin slices as a starter. Also try the lamb hams from the area around the ski resort of Valloire.

There seem to be as many varieties of cured sausages throughout these regions as there are choices of cheese in the whole of France! Isère and Savoie dry sausages are always made with natural casings, slowly aged and never frozen. They are served cold as starters and in salads, added to stews or simply grilled. The most popular include:

saucisses de Magland: cured sausage made with lean pork; typical of the Vallée de l'Arve

diots: small fresh meat sausages, made either solely with lean pork or with a mixture of pork and beef; normally cooked in white wine

caillettes: fresh minced pork sausages with green vegetables

pormoniers de Tarentaise: pork offal with leeks and herbs

saucissons d'ânes: sausages made with donkey meat. Goat meat is also often used

grelots: pork sausages with nuts

salaisons de Savoie: *salaisons* is simply a generic name for charcuterie, taken here to signify specialities from Savoie

Sausages at a regional market

FISH

The clear, pure mountain streams, rivers and lakes provide an important source of protein in the Alpine diet.

char: delicate and succulent lake fish common in the Alpine lakes, particularly Lac d'Annecy

lavaret and féra: commonly encountered as 'whitefish' on English menu translations. Both are the same species (dace) but named differently to distinguish the *lavaret* as the variety from the Lac du Bourget or Lac d'Annecy, and *féra* from Lac Léman. Generally served *à la meunière* (see opposite) or in a light cream sauce

truite: trout; fresh river trout, rather than farmed, is the most prized and is stipulated as such on the menu

omble chevalier: a member of the salmon family, similar to rainbow trout, which lives in deep, cold glacial lakes. A less common, much prized fish with an excellent flavour

VEGETARIAN

It has to be said, vegetarians will have a hard time of it in the mountains, vegans even more so. The concept of vegetarianism still is not fully understood, or acceptably accommodated, even in the largest hotels. You may have to resign yourself to picking through salads and pizzas to remove anchovies, prawns and ham.

Most of the vegetarian options offered depend heavily on salads, eggs and cheese, with the omelette being king. Buffets and self-service restaurants are easiest, but they still rely on meat and fish dishes for main courses; the only vegetarian option again usually being an omelette – charged at the same price as the meat dish.

Crêpes, pasta and pizzas are all reliable options; raclette and fondue are the best regional specialities suitable for vegetarians (see page 31).

COOKING TECHNIQUES

Local recipes have assimilated the techniques and ingredients of neighbouring regions of Savoie, Lyonnais and Bresse, with hints of the Mediterranean; the Italian region of Piedmont (once part of Savoie) has also made a noticeable contribution. The following are a selection of the most popular and representative styles of cooking:

à la meunière: dipped in flour and fried in butter

au gratin: with grated cheese and often breadcrumbs. *Gratin de pommes de terre savoyard* (fine slices of potato and grated Beaufort cheese baked with butter and stock) is an energy-rich local dish

à la bergère: 'shepherd style', generally meaning with ham, mushrooms, onion and very finely cut potatoes

à la bourguignonne: 'Burgundy style', generally meaning casseroled with red wine, onions and mushrooms, but also a style of fondue where meat is dipped in hot oil instead of the Savoie style where hot cheese is the dipping mix. *Fondue bourguignonne* includes a selection of sauces in which to dip the cooked meat

à l'italienne: using pasta and tomatoes

à l'ancienne: prepared to an old, very traditional recipe; used as a generic term with no set ingredients or method of cooking

à la lyonnaise: 'Lyon style', cooked with onions, usually a potato dish

à la niçoise: 'Nice style', usually applied to salad or pizza and including anchovies, tomatoes and olives in the ingredients; with French beans and egg too when referring to the salad

à la vigneron: 'wine grower style', generally any recipe involving wine in its key ingredients

à la crème: made with cream; that is, in a cream sauce

à la dauphinoise: potatoes baked in cream and/or milk, usually served *au gratin*; a classic speciality of the Isère region

> **WELL DONE**
> The French prefer meat rare (*bleu* or *saignante*), so if you prefer it to be well done (*bien cuit*) try asking for it to be very well done (*très bien cuit*), otherwise it is likely to arrive closer to medium (*à point*).

REGIONAL SPECIALITIES

A noble culinary heritage continues to pervade the region's kitchens and restaurants and tongue-twisting, tastebud-teasing local dishes, redolent of the rigours and pleasures of high altitude life, have survived and thrived. Pack your appetite along with your ski gear.

gratin dauphinois: the most emblematic dish of the Isère region. This creamy baked dish of potatoes is mentioned for the first time in the Grenoble city archives (on 12 July 1788) on the menu of an official meal organized by the Duke of Clermont-Tonnerre, Lieutenant General of the Dauphiné. It consists of potatoes, whole milk, cream, salt, pepper, nutmeg, butter and garlic; all but purists now include grated cheese. The potatoes are cooked in the milk and cream, along with the seasonings, before being baked together in the oven to produce a rich and creamy comfort food – perfect as a winter energy booster

raviole: the *raviole* of Dauphiné are small squares of fine pasta, very similar to Italian ravioli, containing a filling of Tomme cheese, eggs and parsley. According to local tradition, proper *raviole* are poached in chicken broth rather than plain water

ganèfles: baked ravioli stuffed with cheese and served in a cream sauce. Bang goes the diet!

farcis: stuffed vegetables (usually minced pork) and cooked in stock
tartiflette: ubiquitous stable of Isère and Savoie chalet kitchens, resembling lasagne in appearance and served for lunch and/or for dinner. A blend of potatoes, Reblochon cheese, lardons, butter, onions, garlic and crème fraîche, oven-baked and served almost bubbling. Traditionally served with charcuterie and pickles. The Savoyard version is traditionally served in a pastry case resembling a large Yorkshire pudding
raclette: a half-wheel of smooth, firm raclette cheese served on a special little heater to melt the cheese, which you scrape off hot on to your plate or bread at the table. Usually served with potatoes and pickles
fondue: in Isère and Savoie this is usually the bread-dipped-in-hot-cheese version, so if you're vegetarian, be sure to order the cheese version rather than the meat-based (*fondue bourguignonne*) one. *Fondue savoyarde* is a blend of two or more cheeses and a little white wine, gently brought to near boiling to liquify, then served at your table in a pot with a flame burner to keep it hot. You are provided with chunks of bread and little spears to dip into the bubbling cheese mixture. Usually served with potatoes and/or salad and charcuterie
pierrade: small strips of meat cooked on a hot slate sprinkled with rock salt, this is usually another DIY task at your table; served with dips and salad
crozets: tiny squares of wheat pasta; sometimes blended with buckwheat flour (*crozets au sarrasin*)
potée savoyarde: stew; usually of ham and vegetables, generally always including Savoy cabbage and potatoes, simmered together but then served separately, with vegetable broth poured over toasted bread

polenta: made from milled corn which is pressed into thick sausage-shapes and used as a carbohydrate-loaded base for a wide range of dishes. Normally associated with the cuisine of the neighbouring Italian regions, but is in fact an ancient and important Savoie speciality. It is easy to store and an important source of energy during the long winter. Traditionally served with sausages or meats in sauce
farcement: similar to terrines and formed by pressing ingredients in a special mould. Recipes vary from village to village, even from house to house, but typically use potatoes and dried fruit grated and kneaded together then pressed into a mould lined with bacon, which is then cooked in a bain-marie for 3–4 hours. The dish is turned out and served in slices and has an unusual sweet-and-sour flavour. A particular favourite during harvests and transhumance periods, as the dish stores well and is packed with energy. The slices can be reheated quickly by sautéing in a pan
gâteau aux noix: walnut cake. A classic dessert of the Isère region, using the famous walnuts of Grenoble; very sweet, but with just the right touch of bitterness from the nuts

MENU

To see the menu, ask for *la carte*, as the 'menu' in France is taken to mean just the daily set menu.
Menu du jour: an economical set menu, usually two or three courses, with at least two choices, often with dessert, bread and sometimes even water and/or table wine included

Walnut cake, an Isère favourite for those with a sweet tooth

CHARTREUSE
Sotanum

MOUNTAIN SPORTS NUTRITION

Don't make the mistake of regarding eating on snowsports holidays as merely pit stops for refuelling: a couple of beers and a hamburger won't help you nail that three-sixty or give you the legs to progress into that fresh powder after lunch!

Nutritious, warming meals with quality, fresh ingredients and frequent non-alcoholic fluid intake are what your body craves at altitude. Remember, you are in an Arctic environment participating in a demanding sport. This requires an athletic-minded approach to diet. Far better to supply your body with optimum nutrition while, since you're on holiday, allowing yourself a more gourmet event. If you had a racehorse worth millions, you wouldn't feed it beer and hamburgers! So why treat yourself as any less worthy?

SUGGESTED SNOWSPORTS DIET

Breakfast: a 'Continental' breakfast of coffee, croissant and cigarette just isn't adequate to support a morning in the mountains – you need slow-release energy-rich foods such as muesli, bread with cheese or ham, honey and yogurt
Lunch: light, warm dishes based on pasta, rice or vegetables with meat or fish to supply plenty of complex carbohydrate energy, protein and fibre
Dinner: salad, soup or vegetables, followed by fish, fowl or light meat – don't make it too hearty as a heavy meal will interfere with your sleep
Snacks: fruit or yogurt or a sandwich or dried fruits/nuts
Drinks: fruit juice, tea (herbal is best), hot chocolate, water and more water

WINE

A giant in the oenological world, France needs no preamble regarding the quality of its wines.

The Isère region, though, is not a noted wine-growing region, with only the ancient Gallo-Roman area around the town of Vienne, just south of Lyon, beginning to emerge again as a serious wine-producing area. These ancient vineyards, situated on granite hillsides overlooking the town, had been abandoned along with many others in the region during the first half of the 20th century, following the phylloxera infestation which proved so widespread and devastating in Europe at that time. Isère's recently reborn wines, mostly produced with Syrah grapes, are still developing and should continue to improve as the new vines age. The wines tend to be strong: Sotanum and Taburnum are the names to look out for, particularly in regional speciality shops and delicatessens.

The Savoie region has been producing wine since Roman times and were referred to by Pliny (AD 23–79), who named them as the wines of Allobrogie; *vin de pays d'Allobrogie* is now the name used for good-quality table wines produced outside the AOC boundaries. The region boasts a diversity of terrain: from mountain foothills, river valleys and sunny lake shores.

The rich alluvial land of the Combe de Savoie in particular is a major wine producing area, boasting a number of world-class, yet relatively little-known labels, although the vast majority of wine produced in the region is for local consumption.

Mostly, Savoie wines are subtle whites. They should be drunk young and go very well with the delicate lake fish and creamy local cheeses; they are also used extensively in cooking, featuring as a key ingredient in *fondue savoyarde* to help liquify the cheese.

There are four principal AOCs and 22 Crus in Savoie: the AOCs are Vin de Savoie; Roussette de Savoie; Crépy; and Seyssel, which is the oldest of the AOCs, first awarded in 1942. All have the distinctive cross of Savoie moulded just below the neck of the bottle. The Vin de Savoie AOC is subdivided into Abymes, Apremont, Arbin, Ayze, Bergeron, Chautagne, Chignin, Cruet, Jongieux, Marignan, Marin, Montmélian, Ripaille, St Jean de la Porte, St Jeoire Prieuré and Pétillant de Savoie. The Roussette de Savoie AOC is subdivided into Frangy, Marestel, Monterminod and Monthoux.

Apremont, a classic Savoie white

No fewer than 23 different varieties of grape are cultivated; three times more whites than reds, as the whites are best suited to the chalky soil.

WHITES

Jacquère: predominates in the Combe de Savoie and Les Abymes areas, used in Apremont and Abymes wines. Light dry white, with a very delicate yellow tint

Bergeron: almost exclusively grown in the Chignin Cru communes

Altesse: most common in the Seyssel and Frangy terroirs and used in AOC Roussette de Savoie. Legend states that a Cypriot royal introduced this variety from her homeland on her visit to Savoie

Chasselas: predominantly grown in the regions nearest to the Swiss border

Roussanne: mainly cultivated in the Chignin Cru

REDS

Mondeuse: the most prevalent Savoie red, mostly grown in the Combe de Savoie area. Produces wines with a rich purple-red hue, with a bouquet of strawberry, raspberry and violet. Good accompaniment with charcuterie

Pinot Noir: the classic red grape of Burgundy; here, some is used in the Chignin Vin de Savoie reds

Gamay: classic old-world vine (Beaujolais-lovers will recognize its fruity style) cultivated for its reliability

FRENCH WINE TERMS

Appellation d'Origine Contrôlée (AOC): the premier quality control, protected by law, awarded to the highest quality wines in specifically demarcated areas

Vin Délimité de Qualité Supérieure (VDQS): quality award just below full AOC

Vin de Pays: followed by the name of the département it comes from. Local table wine

Vin Doux Natural (VDN): naturally sweet wine (dessert wine).

cru: there are two distinct meanings to this term – it is used to refer to the specific territory where the wine comes from, but is also used as a standard of classification and is normally encountered with champagnes and fine wines which take the terms Premier Cru, Grand Cru and Premier Grand Cru, denoting the very highest quality wines

en carafe: decanted into a carafe, usually a half-litre or litre

en pichet: decanted into a jug; usually a small one, but available in various sizes to suit the number of people at your table

sec: dry; **moëlleux**: sweet; **pétillant** (or **perlé**): slightly sparkling; **mousseux**: sparkling

VIN CHAUD

Hot mulled wine. Ubiquitous après-ski warmer in Alpine ski resorts.

Recipe: *1 bottle (75 cl) red Vin de Savoie, 115 g (4 oz) sugar, 1 lemon, sprig of thyme, bay leaf, clove.*

Heat the wine and sugar in a saucepan; when the froth begins to form, remove from the heat, add the lemon (thinly sliced), and other ingredients. Return to the heat and allow to boil for no more than two minutes. Serve hot.

APERITIFS & DIGESTIFS

Chartreuse: the most famous regional product from Isère, with a recorded history stretching back 400 years and made to a secret recipe by the monks from the Grande-Chartreuse monastery at Voiron, north of Grenoble. Green Chartreuse (55° proof) is the strongest; added to hot chocolate it is a delicious après-ski warmer. Yellow Chartreuse (40° proof) is sweeter and softer, it is made with the same plants as the green variety, but in different proportions

génépy: a generic term for all regional spirits using Alpine wormwood plant in their flavouring. The liqueur is served as an aperitif and/or digestif and is used to flavour pastries and desserts

Gentian liqueur: flavoured with the intensely blue-coloured flower of the Alpine Gentian

liqueur de noix: liqueur made using the famous Grenoble walnuts; another product of the monastery of Grande-Chartreuse

antésite: a non-alcoholic concentrate of liquorice which you add to mineral water. First introduced over a century ago by a pharmacist from Voiron, and used to aid digestion

LIGHTER DRINKS

bière: beer. Most of the beers available in resort bars are standard international brews sold from the tap. However, the Brasserie Artisanale du Dauphiné is a notable local producer from Grenoble; look out for their walnut-flavoured beer named 'Mandrin' after this region's own version of Robin Hood

café: with breakfast, as a mid-morning and afternoon pick-me-up, after dinner and at just about any other social encounter, a coffee is as much of a national institution in France as 'a nice cup of tea' is in the UK. The variations in preference are wide ranging: *décaféiné* is decaf; *café crème* is made with milk or cream and is more commonly referred to as *café au lait*; *café noir* is a small black coffee; *café express* is espresso. *Café crème/café au lait* is traditionally only drunk at breakfast time by the French, but at any time of day by tourists

tisane: herbal infusion; this is the generic term in French for any herbal tea

eau: water. The Alps have a plethora of natural springs which are the source of many brands of bottled water. Regionally, most comes from the Haute Savoie, from the springs at the foot of the Alps on the southern shores of Lac Léman, but bottled water from the spa town of Aix-les-Bains on the Lac du Bourget is an excellent local mineral water.

There are various types to choose from: *eau gazeuse* is sparkling; *eau plate* is still; *eau nature* is plain tap water; *eau minérale* is mineral water, such as Perrier or Evian, each from a specific source and high in mineral content and often with quite a distinct, even salty, taste.

Although tap water quality is generally excellent, it is safest to drink only bottled water.

DELICATESSENS & GOURMET SHOPS

Chez le Gaulois Regional products boutique with a café-bar for those who just can't wait to taste the wares: local and Savoie cheeses, local honey, charcuterie, preserves and génépy; raclette and fondues to take away, with fondue sets and raclette heaters available to loan. ⓐ 70 avenue de la Muzelle

Le Fin Gourmet Excellent butchers, also stocking a wide range of charcuterie, cheeses and other regional produce; roast chickens, raclettes and fondues to take away, with fondue sets and raclette heaters available to loan. ⓐ 23 place de Venosc

Le Vieux Chalet Large regional products shop with a wide range of fine wines and regional liqueurs; charcuterie, cheeses, honey and preserves. ⓐ 85 avenue de la Muzelle

La Marjolaine Quality chocolaterie and patisserie with its own salon de thé and a nice range of speciality ice creams. ⓐ 114 avenue de la Muzelle

Au Terroir One of the quaint boutiques in the artisans village at Venosc; selling regional products including chesses, hams, preserves and liqueurs; fresh bread and basic provisions too, perfect for a picnic in the valley.

Miellerie des Ecrins Another of the little boutiques in the charming artisans village at Venosc; specializes in honey and apiculture products such as soaps and creams, sweets and salad dressings.

LANGUAGE
Phrasebook

PARLEZ-VOUS FRANÇAIS? DO YOU SPEAK FRENCH?

Having even a basic insight into the language of the country you are visiting will help enormously in getting the maximum enjoyment from your stay; allowing you to engage more readily with your hosts and speeding up assistance if you need it.

Of course, French is the official language of the region, but most of the tourism service personnel you will encounter will speak and understand some English.

The following is a selection of useful words and phrases most frequently needed on a snowsports holiday:

ENGLISH	FRENCH
Hello	*Bonjour*
Good morning	*Bonjour*
Good afternoon	*Bon après-midi*
Good evening	*Bonsoir*
Good night	*Bon nuit*
Goodbye	*Au revoir*
See you soon	*À bientôt*
Please	*S'il vous plaît*
Thank you	*Merci*
Yes	*Oui*
No	*Non*
How are you?	*Comment allez-vous?*
Very well thank you	*Très bien merci*
I don't understand	*Je ne comprends pas*
Sorry	*Pardon*
How much?	*C'est combien?*
Give me...	*Donnez-moi...*
Where is?	*Où est?*
Where are?	*Où sont?*
When?	*Quand?*
Why?	*Pourquoi?*
Open	*Ouvert*
Closed	*Fermé*

ENGLISH	FRENCH
Monday	*Lundi*
Tuesday	*Mardi*
Wednesday	*Mercredi*
Thursday	*Jeudi*
Friday	*Vendredi*
Saturday	*Samedi*
Sunday	*Dimanche*
Winter	*L'hiver*
Summer	*L'été*
One	*Un*
Two	*Deux*
Three	*Trois*
Four	*Quatre*
Five	*Cinq*
Six	*Six*
Seven	*Sept*
Eight	*Huit*
Nine	*Neuf*
Ten	*Dix*
Eleven	*Onze*

ENGLISH	FRENCH
Twelve	*Douze*
Thirteen	*Treize*
Fourteen	*Quatorze*
Fifteen	*Quinze*
Sixteen	*Seize*
Seventeen	*Dix-sept*
Eighteen	*Dix-huit*
Nineteen	*Dix-neuf*
Twenty	*Vingt*
Thirty	*Trente*
Forty	*Quarante*
Fifty	*Cinquante*
Sixty	*Soixante*
Seventy	*Soixante-dix*
Eighty	*Quatre-vingts*
Ninety	*Quatre-vingt-dix*
Hundred	*Cent*
First	*Le premier*
Second	*Le deuxième*
Third	*Le troisième*

ENGLISH	FRENCH
PHRASES	
Do you speak English?	*Parlez-vous anglais?*
What time is it?	*Quelle heure est-il?*
I would like	*Je voudrais*
Could you show me	*Pouvez-vous me l'indiquer*
Could you help me	*Pouvez-vous m'aider*
Where are the toilets?	*Où sont les toilettes?*
I've lost...	*J'ai perdu...*
ACCIDENTS / SICKNESS / EMERGENCIES	
I don't feel well	*Je ne me sens pas bien*
I've had a fall	*Je suis tombé*
I'm dizzy	*J'ai des vertiges*
It hurts here	*J'ai mal ici*
There's been an accident	*Il y a eu un accident*
Doctor	*Médicin*
Dentist	*Dentiste*

ENGLISH	FRENCH
ACCIDENTS / SICKNESS / EMERGENCIES (CONTINUED)	
Head	*Tête*
Arm	*Bras*
Wrist	*Poignet*
Hand	*Main*
Leg	*Jambe*
Ankle	Cheville
Foot	*Pied*
Eye	*Oeil*
Ear	*Oreille*
Condom	*Préservatif*
Suncream	*Crème solaire*
Tampons	*Tampons*
I've got...	*Je souffre de...*
Constipation	*Constipation*
Diarrhoea	*Diarrhée*
Stomach ache	*Mal d'estomac*
Sunstroke	*Coup de soleil*
Headache	*Mal de tête*
Earache	*Mal d'oreille*
DIRECTIONS & PLACES	
Left	*À gauche*
Right	*À droite*
Straight ahead	*Tout droit*
I've lost my way	*Je me suis égaré*
Supermarket	*Supermarché*
Tourist information	*Office de tourisme*
Phonebox	*Cabine téléphonique*
Post office	*La poste*
Post box	*Boîte aux lettres*
Postage stamp	*Timbre*
AT THE RESTAURANT	
Do you have a menu in English?	*Vous avez un menu en anglais?*
The wine list	*La carte des vins*
Dish of the day	*Plat du jour*
The bill	*L'addition*
Bottle	*Bouteille*

ENGLISH	FRENCH
AT THE RESTAURANT (CONTINUED)	
Corkscrew	*Tire-bouchon*
Toothpick	*Cure-dent*
Tumbler	*Verre*
Wineglass	*Verre*
Rosé	*Vin rosé*
Red wine	*Vin rouge*
White wine	*Vin blanc*
Beer	*Bière*
Draught beer	*Bière pression*
Water	*Eau*
White coffee	*Café au lait*
Beef	*Boeuf*
Bread	*Pain*
Butter	*Beurre*
Cheese	*Fromage*
Chicken	*Poulet*
Dessert	*Déssert*
Egg	*Oeuf*
Fish	*Poisson*
Ice cream	*Glace*
Lamb	*Agneau*
Meat	*Viande*
Poultry	*Volaille*
Roast	*Rôti*
Salad	*Salade*
Soup	*Potage*
Vegetables	*Légumes*
SKI TERMS	
I'd like a ski pass	*Je voudrais un forfait de ski*
To rent	*Louer*
To ice skate/ice skates	*Patiner/Patins à glace*
Avalanche	*Avalanche*
Bindings	*Fixations*
Cable car	*Téléphérique*
Chair lift	*Télésiège*
Cross-country skiing	*Ski de fond*
Drag lift	*Téléski*
Gloves	*Gants*

ENGLISH	FRENCH
SKI TERMS (CONTINUED)	
Goggles	*Lunettes de ski*
Gondola	*Télécabine*
Mountain	*Montagne*
Passport photo	*Photo d'identité*
Ski boots	*Chaussures de ski*
Ski lessons	*Leçons de ski*
Ski poles	*Bâtons de ski*
Ski wax	*Fart à ski*
Skis	*Skis*
Socks	*Chaussettes*
Snowchains	*Les chaînes de neige*

TEMP:													
	°C	−25	−20	−15	−10	−5	0	5	10	15	20	25	30
	°F	−13	−4	5	14	23	32	41	50	59	68	77	86

CONVERSIONS

DISTANCES

Centimetres to inches	x 0.394
Inches to centimetres	x 2.540
Yards to metres	x 0.914
Metres to yards	x 1.094
Miles to kilometres	x 1.609
Kilometres to miles	x 0.621

AREA

Acres to hectares	x 0.405
Hectares to acres	x 2.471

HEIGHT

Metres to feet	x 3.281
Feet to metres	x 0.305

ACCURACY

Conversion formulas are rounded up to 3 decimal places, therefore, calculations may result in slight differences in practice.

HEALTH & SAFETY

Piste security

PREPARATION FOR SNOWSPORTS

It is all too easy in these times of low-cost travel and rapid communications to forget that you are travelling from a relatively benign temperate climate straight into Arctic conditions. Furthermore, you are going to be careering around this wild and inhospitable environment standing on two planks or a tray, moving at the speed of a car with not much more than a knitted beanie and a pair of padded gloves to protect you!

The only way to ensure your safety and get maximum enjoyment out of your trip is to have respect for the seriousness of the situation you are putting yourself in and prepare accordingly.

Preparation begins at home: join a gym, ride a bike or just walk further and more often. The best and safest skiers and snowboarders are fit ones.

Once in your resort, warm-up at the start of each day and after rest breaks. A few minutes' stretching and/or jogging on the spot will pay dividends in your ability to sustain activity and avoid injury.

Weather conditions in the high mountains change rapidly and dramatically, so dress for all eventualities – it is easier to cool down than it is to warm up. Most heat loss occurs through your head, so always wear a hat. In the snow parks and when freeriding, wear a helmet – all the best riders do.

ESSENTIAL ITEMS

Carry the following items with you on the mountain:

- water
- sunblock for skin and lips
- a piste map
- spare clothing
- high-energy snacks
- basic first-aid kit

PROTECTING YOURSELF FROM THE EFFECTS OF ALTITUDE

Temperature is inversely proportional to altitude: the higher you go, the lower the temperature drops.

Every 100 m (328 ft) rise in altitude above sea level equates to a shift north of around 161 km (100 miles). By the time you get up to 2500 m (8203 ft) that's equivalent to going from London to the Arctic Circle.

Conversely, the sun's radiation increases with altitude. For every 100 metres you go up, solar UV intensifies by about two per cent; so at 2500 metres you are being fried twice as quickly as you would be on a Mediterranean beach.

On overcast and snowy days, the clouds only disperse the UV-rays but do not stop them. Sunscreens absorb a set percentage of the UV reaching you; only a total sunblock and technical eyewear will provide maximum protection. Do not forget that snow reflects the sunlight and UV-rays – make sure you protect under your chin, below and behind your ears, under your nose and your eyelids. Goggles provide all-round protection and enhanced visibility; sunglasses are fine for wearing on the terraces or strolling around a resort, but they are not sportswear. Wearing a hat not only keeps you warm, but protects you from sunstroke too.

Dehydration is a problem in all active sports. When you add an increase in altitude to the equation, the problem becomes compounded and potentially fatal. Dehydration leads to fatigue, and tiredness is the primary cause of most accidents, injury and hypothermia. The best way to ensure that you are well hydrated is to start that way and maintain a good fluid balance throughout the day. The trick is to sip water or isotonic fluids little and often. Invest in a hydration backpack or carry a couple of bottles of water with you.

GEAR SAFETY

Ski boots were not designed for walking on the piste. On steep slopes it is always safer to keep your skis or snowboard on. If you take them off and there is ice underfoot you will have even less control than you had with your gear on.

When you do take your gear off, make sure that it is secured. If your skis or board slide away they can severely injure or even kill someone in just the few seconds it takes for them to pick up velocity. Legally you are responsible: this is not an accident but an avoidable lack of care.

Put your gear in a rack if there is one available. If not, make sure you set your board down upside down so that your bindings dig into the snow. Skis should be set down with their brake legs digging into the snow or placed upright and rammed deep into the snow where they can't run away if they fall over. Do not lean gear on the sides of cable car cabins or on flat walls. It will slide off and knock others with them and they are just like a guillotine when they crash down.

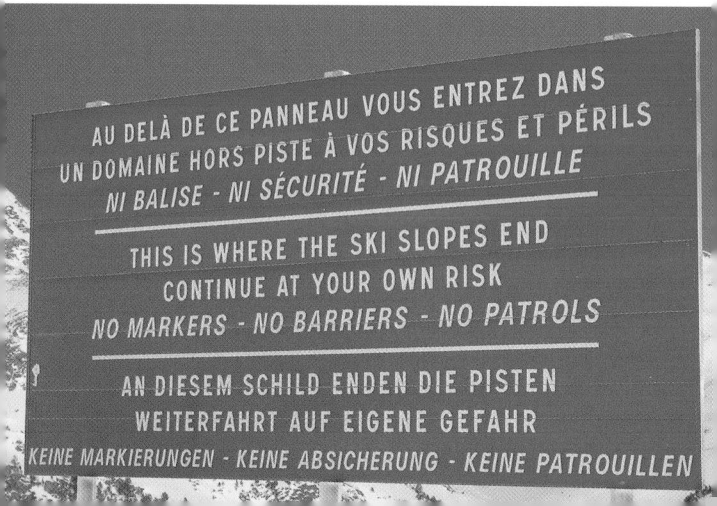

AVALANCHE RISK WARNINGS

Plain yellow flag = risk levels 1 to 2:
low to moderate probability of avalanche

Chequered yellow and black flag = risk levels 3 to 4:
moderate to high probability of avalanche

Black flag = risk level 5:
absolute risk of large avalanche

Zero risk does not exist! Always be aware and prepared.

OFF-PISTE

Check if your insurance policy covers off-piste skiing then follow these rules for optimum safety:

- Never leave the marked ski area on your own; it is safest to travel in groups of three persons minimum.
- Unless you know the area like the back of your hand, always employ a qualified mountain guide.
- Never blindly follow someone else's tracks, they may lead in the wrong direction or even off a cliff!
- Always carry the essential off-piste kit: avalanche transceiver, shovel, probe, map and compass.

If travelling off-piste in glacial areas you should also carry a climbing rope, harness, ice screws, carabiners and rope ascenders/foot slings. However, these items are only effective if you know what they are for and how to use them properly. Many resorts run avalanche awareness and safety equipment training courses. The golden rule is: get wise or get lost!

Piste signs and markers have been put there by mountain professionals – respect them! They are there to protect you and others too

SLOPE RULES & REGULATIONS

The International Ski Federation (FIS) has set rules for slope users, which have established a legal precedent. Failure to abide by these rules may result in your ski pass being annulled and you may be banned from using the installations and the slopes. If you cause injury or death you may also be charged with negligence or manslaughter. The following is a summary:

1. Slope users must not endanger others.
2. You must adapt speed and behaviour to your ability and to current conditions.
3. The slope user in front always has priority.
4. When overtaking, leave room for those in front to manoeuvre.
5. Check uphill and downhill before you enter, start or cross pistes.
6. Only stop at the sides of the piste. If you have fallen, clear the slope quickly.
7. When moving up or down on foot, keep to the side of the piste.
8. Respect all piste signs and station information.
9. In the case of accidents, always give assistance.
10. You must give your identity to the Piste Patrol, Emergency Services and other accident victims when requested.

INSURANCE

Accident insurance is not included in ski pass prices. Make sure you are adequately covered or take the insurance supplement. Never travel without comprehensive winter sports travel insurance and always ensure that you are covered for on-mountain rescue and transport to hospital, on top of medical treatment and hospitalization cover. Some sports, such as paragliding and snowmobiling, are not covered by standard ski insurance and you will need to take out extra cover for these.

LES DEUX ALPES
Resort & ski area

INTRODUCTION

Les Deux Alpes (now more commonly written as Les 2 Alpes) is one of the biggest and most important ski stations in France's Isère département. It occupies a lively linear plateau, high between the Romanche and Vénéon valleys on the edge of the wild and beautiful Parc National des Ecrins, at the latitude where the Northern and Southern Alps meet.

In the regional dialect, the word 'alpe' refers to a high meadow; Les Deux Alpes gets its name from the fact that it straddles both ends of the mountain pastures between the two nearby parish villages of Mont-de-Lans and Venosc, whose originally separate summer-only farm settlements have now merged into one large, year-round, international mountain-sports resort, strung out along these sun-drenched meadows.

The ski station is consistently at the vanguard of new-school snowsports and has one of the biggest Snow Parks in the Alps and innovative in-bounds freeride features marketed under the 'Slide' banner. The ski area is most famous for having Europe's largest skiable glacier; with high-altitude, snow-sure pistes which are just as busy in summer as they are in winter; the descent from the summit to the lowest piste-accessible point in the ski domain also delivers an incredible on-piste vertical drop of 2220 m (7282 ft), still one of the world's biggest.

PRONUNCIATION

Les Deux Alpes Lay-dous-alp **Le Bourg-d'Oisans** Luh-borg-waz-on

Les Deux Alpes, centre of the Slide universe

Les Deux Alpes is a large and lively town, with over 2000 permanent inhabitants; this figure swells 16-fold during the height of the winter ski season when combined with the influx of snowsports visitors, lending an animated ambiance to the resort. There is plenty of room to spread out though, since the town sprawls for almost 2 km (1¼ miles) in an uninterrupted strip along the base of its town slopes. It offers a wide choice of accommodation and a large and vibrant selection of bars, restaurants and shops; the resort does have an unpolished feel, but it has a discernible soul.

The two parish villages, in their respective valleys below either end of the col holding Les Deux Alpes, have an authentic l'Oisans character which is still redolent of times gone by, both are linked by ski lift with Les Deux Alpes, accessible on foot by all visitors (Pedestrian Pass required for non-skiers – see page 76). Non-skiers can also access all of the main lift and piste interchanges in the ski area, which serve as the service hubs for the on-mountain bars/restaurants, making this a good choice for mixed ability groups who will also appreciate the resort's good range of alternative activities and visitor attractions.

The ski area is mostly characterized by long well-groomed cruising pistes well above the tree-line and, in a reflection of the linear form of the town, flows in a predominately long and narrow fashion along the backbone of glacial ridges which dominate this landscape. Despite the narrow shape of the ski area, the domain is big enough to house a respectably wide range of terrain: all the way from sheltered birch woods to glacial summits, and ranging from easily accessible beginners' slopes to seriously exposed off-piste itineraries.The individual sectors that make up the ski domain each offer a different flavour to each day's skiing.

The **Pied Moutet sector** was the resort's first to be developed but now feels remote from the core ski area, a real feature when you want to escape the crowds.

The **Crêtes/Diable sectors** cover the ridges above the main town slopes and house the challenging and almost exclusively black-graded home runs, but these intertwined sectors are accessible to all and house some good excursions for beginners too.

The **Toura/La Fée sectors** have a wilder edge, Toura features Les Deux Alpes' excellent Snow Park and has a buzzing atmosphere; La Fée is at the quieter margins of the domain and is filled with (until now) secret stashes of freeride joy.

The **Glacier sector** is the highest and most exposed of the sectors, but the domed shaped summits allow beginners and intermediates to go as high as any advanced ability visitors can. As well as offering guaranteed snow and hosting the station's enjoyable Slide zones, this sector also opens up a myriad of off-piste routes and links into La Grave.

Les Deux Alpes has one of Europe's clearest piste maps; every lift is clearly numbered and there are masses of piste map and information displays scattered throughout the domain, making it very easy to quickly move between all sectors.

FURTHER INFORMATION

- Les Deux Alpes tourist office: current information and an excellent resort guide. ⓣ +33 (0)4 76 79 22 00 ⓦ www.les2alpes.com
- Radio Europe 2 Les 2 Alpes 96.2 FM: on-site weather, snow reports, events and information, plus music.

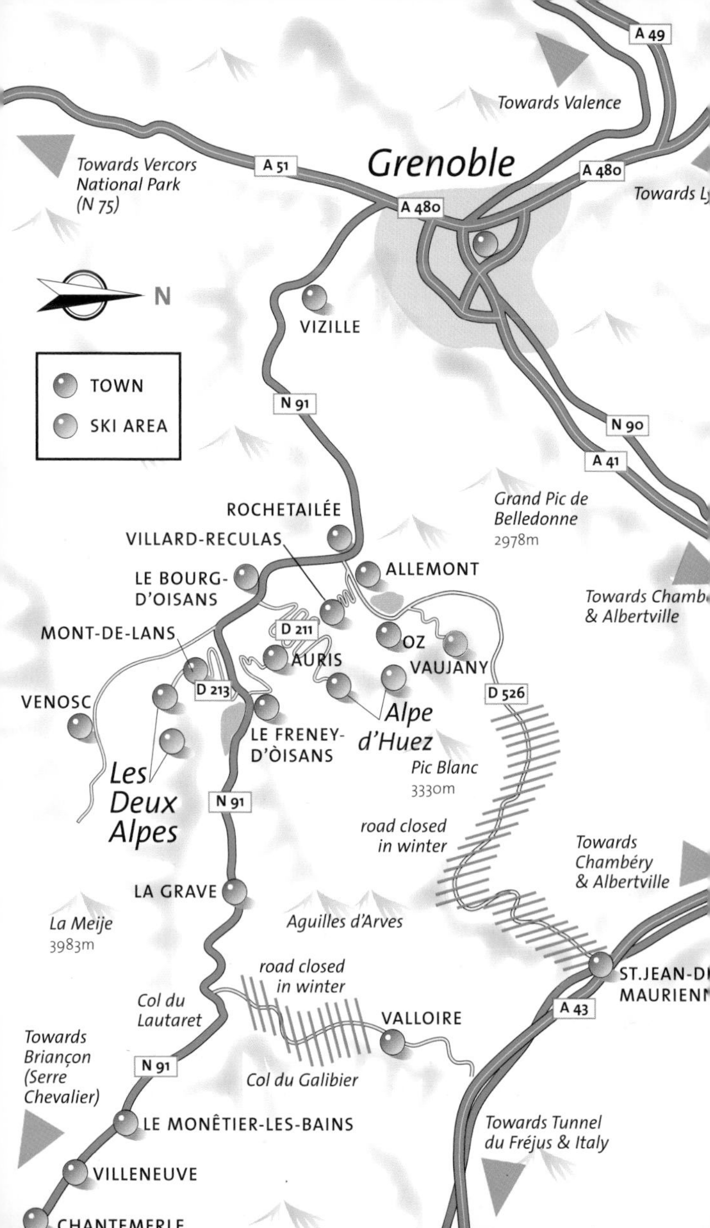

A 49
Towards Valence
Towards Vercors
National Park
(N 75)
A 51
Grenoble
A 480
A 480
Towards Ly
N
VIZILLE
TOWN
SKI AREA
N 91
N 90
A 41
Grand Pic de
Belledonne
2978m
ROCHETAILÉE
VILLARD-RECULAS
LE BOURG-
D'OISANS
ALLEMONT
Towards Chamb
& Albertville
MONT-DE-LANS
D 211
OZ
AURIS
VAUJANY
D 213
D 526
VENOSC
Alpe
d'Huez
LE FRENEY-
D'ÒISANS
Pic Blanc
3330m
Les
Deux
Alpes
N 91
road closed
in winter
Towards
Chambéry
& Albertville
LA GRAVE
La Meije
3983m
Aguilles d'Arves
ST.JEAN-D
MAURIEN
road closed
in winter
Col du
Lautaret
A 43
VALLOIRE
Towards
Briançon
(Serre
Chevalier)
N 91
Col du Galibier
LE MONÊTIER-LES-BAINS
Towards Tunnel
du Fréjus & Italy
VILLENEUVE
CHANTEMERLE

COMING & GOING

Les Deux Alpes and its surrounding villages all lie close to le Bourg-d'Oisans, the compact capital of l'Oisans. The only access route in winter is the main N91 road along the Romanche valley between Grenoble and Briançon; the route from Briançon crosses the high altitude and frequently snowbound Col du Lautaret near La Grave, making the route from Grenoble the principal one.

Daily coach transfers are available from central Grenoble and regularly from most of the nearest international airports. For further details go to www.vfd.fr and www.satobus-alpes.com

You can also fly straight in to the town's helipad: contact SAF Helicopters ⓣ +33 (0)4 76 79 75 01

By road from Grenoble: take the A480 autoroute south, straight through Grenoble, and leave at exit no. 8, signed 'Vizille-Stations de l'Oisans', on to the N91. The N91 bypasses the town of Vizille and continues towards le Bourg-d'Oisans. 25 km (15½ miles) after Vizille, you come to the hamlet of Rochetailée and a turn off to the left towards Allemont for the Grandes Rousses satellite stations of Villard-Reculas, Oz-en-Oisans and Vaujany; bear right and continue on the N91 for a further 7 km (4½ miles) towards le Bourg-d'Oisans.

Once at le Bourg-d'Oisans, continue straight though the town on the N91; the left-hand turn-off for Alpe d'Huez is at the first major junction, just 1.2 km (¾ mile) beyond Bourg-d'Oisans; bear right to bypass this and continue on the N91, following the signs for Briançon and Les Deux Alpes. The right-hand turn off for **Venosc** (on to the D530) is a further 4.8 km (3 miles) along this main road; Venosc village is then just 7 km (4¼ miles) along the Vénéon valley; otherwise, stay on the N91 for **Les Deux Alpes**.

The main N91 now enters the impressive and precipitous Gorges de l'Infernet (Gorges of Hell), climbing a steep and narrow route cut into the sheer cliffs above the torrent course of the Romanche river – stay alert for rock falls and black ice. Emerging from the tunnels at the top, you immediately come to a junction at the Lac du Chambon dam: for **La Grave**, turn left across the top of the dam to remain on the N91, signed for the Col du Lautaret and Briançon – La Grave is 14 km (8¾ miles) further on straddling this main route; for **Mont-de-Lans** and **Les Deux Alpes**, turn right on to the D213. Mont-de-Lans is just 4.5 km (2¾ miles) ahead, Les Deux Alpes 7.5 km beyond that.

Approaching Les Deux Alpes, you pass under a pisted foot-bridge and arrive at the place de Mont-de-Lans roundabout in the Alpe de Mont-de-Lans quarter: turn left for Les Deux Alpes 1800 quarter; or, continue straight ahead for the resort centre and Alpe de Venosc quarter (see town plans on pages 63 and 65).

⓿ Please note that it is obligatory to carry snowchains on all these approach roads, except the autoroute.

DISTANCES TO LES DEUX ALPES

• Le Bourg-d'Oisans	26 km (16¼ miles)
• Grenoble	76 km (47½ miles)
• Lyon	176 km (110 miles)
• Chambéry	53 km (95½ miles)
• Geneva	233 km (145½ miles)

➊ *Place de Mont-de-Lans, entering Les Deux Alpes*

Parking: to deal with the massive influx of winter visitors, Les Deux Alpes has provided free-of-charge open car parks, roadside parking bays and pay-to-use covered car parks at various locations around the resort, generally beside the main lifts bases (see town plans on pages 63 and 65).

LES DEUX ALPES (MONT-DE-LANS QUARTER) TOWN PLAN

KEY

- Information office
- Gondola lift
- Chair lift
- Main bus stop
- ATM cash machine
- Ski pass sales point
- Equipment hire shop
- Pharmacy
- Medical centre
- Post office
- Supermarket
- Car park

HOTELS & APARTMENTS

1. Hotel Mercure
2. Club Med
3. Hotel des Marmottes
4. MMV Aparthotel
5. Hotel La Carlina
6. Hotel La Béranère
7. Hotel Edelweiss
8. Hotel Souleil'Or
9. Hotel La Brunerie
10. Hotel Le Sherpa

RESTAURANTS

1. Tribeca Caffé
2. Le Rouge et Noir

BARS & CLUBS

1. L'Opera nightclub
2. O'Brian's
3. Le Windsor

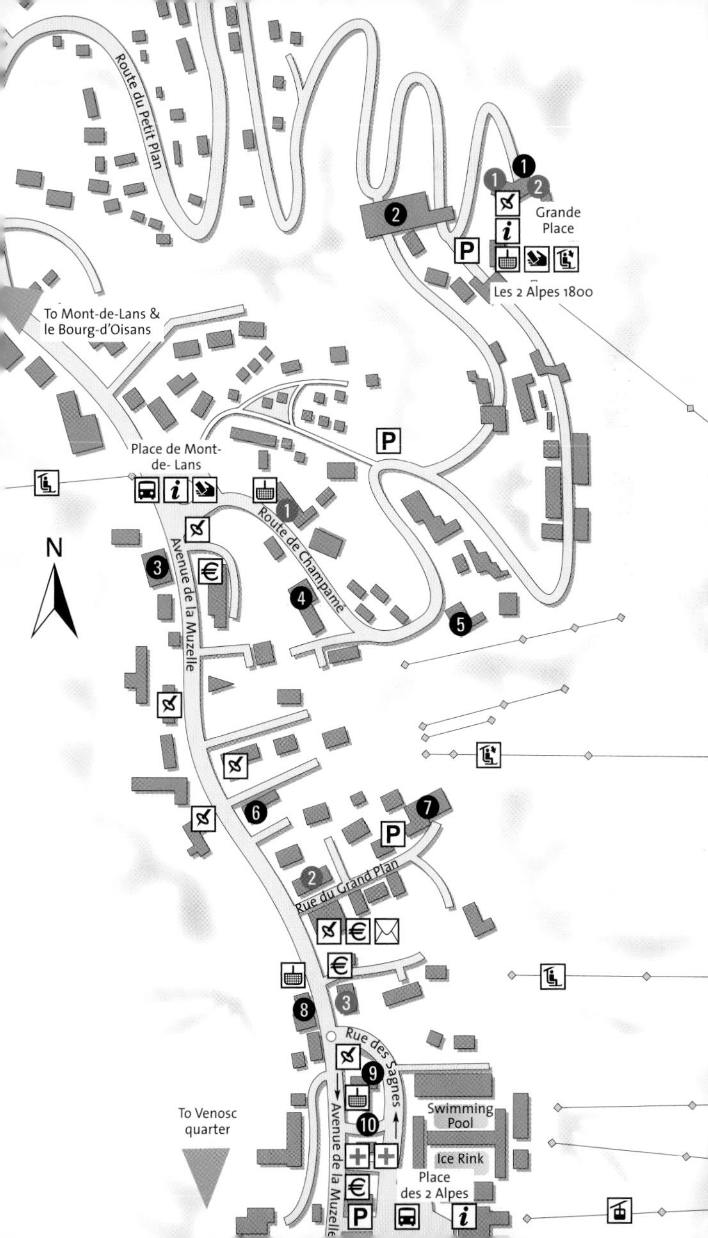

Route du Petit Plan
Grande Place
Les 2 Alpes 1800
To Mont-de-Lans & le Bourg-d'Oisans
Place de Mont-de- Lans
Route de Champamé
Avenue de la Muzelle
N
Rue du Grand Plan
Rue des Sagnes
To Venosc quarter
Swimming Pool
Ice Rink
Place des 2 Alpes
Avenue de la Muzelle

LES DEUX ALPES (VENOSC) TOWN PLAN

KEY

- Information office
- Gondola lift
- Chair lift
- Main bus stop
- ATM cash machine
- Ski pass sales point
- Equipment hire shop
- Pharmacy
- Medical centre
- Post office
- Supermarket
- Car park

HOTELS & APARTMENTS

1. Hotel Touring
2. Hotel Lutins
3. Hotel Aux Alpiniste
4. Hotel La Meije
5. Hotel Le Crêt
6. Hotel Côte Brune
7. Hotel L'Aalbourg
8. Hotel Les Mélèzes
9. Hotel La Belle Etoile
10. Hotel L'Aiglon
11. Hotel Les Airelles
12. Hotel Le Chalet Mounier

RESTAURANTS

1. Crêperie de La Meije
2. Les Sagnes
3. Les Bleuets
4. L'Étable
5. Le Cellier
6. Bel'Auberge

BARS & CLUBS

1. Slide Planet
2. Le Pressoir
3. The Lounge
4. L'Avalanche nightclub
5. La Grotte du Yeti
6. Barrio Alto

N
To Mont-de-Lans qtr.
Mont-de-Lans &
Le Bourg-d'Oisans
Rue des Sagnes
Avenue de la Muzelle
Swimming Pool
Ice Rink
Place des 2 Alpes
Place de la Croix des Limites
Rue des Vikings
Rue du Rouchas
Rue du Cairou
Rue Saint Claude
Rue Sainte Luce
Place de Alpe de Venosc
Gondola lift to Venosc Village

SKI AREA DATA

• Opening time	08.45 hours
• Last lift up	17.00 hours
• Skiable area	1,120 hectares (453½ acres)
• Altitude	1300–3600 m (4265–11,812 ft)
• Vertical drop	2300 m (7546 ft)
• Access points	10
• Ski schools	10

• Ski lifts	51		
Funiculars	*1*	*Non-declutchable chair lifts*	*16*
Cable cars	*3*	*Declutchable chair lift*	*7*
Gondolas	*3*	*Button lifts*	*19*
Inclined elevators	*1*	*Rope tows*	*1*
(Free lifts	*4)*		
• Capacity	71,767 passengers/hour		

• Pistes	102 (= 220 km/137 miles)		
Green	*27*	*Snow parks*	*1*
Blue	*45*	*Halfpipes*	*1*
Red	*17*	*Children's*	*3*
Black	*13*	*Nordic*	*20 km/12 3/4 miles*
		Freestyle zones	*4*

• Hands-free ski pass	No
• Snowmaking	191 cannons (covering 47 ha/19 acres of pistes)
• First-aid posts	7
• Medical centres	2
• Mountain bars/restaurants	9 sites
• Visitor information	www.les2alpes.com

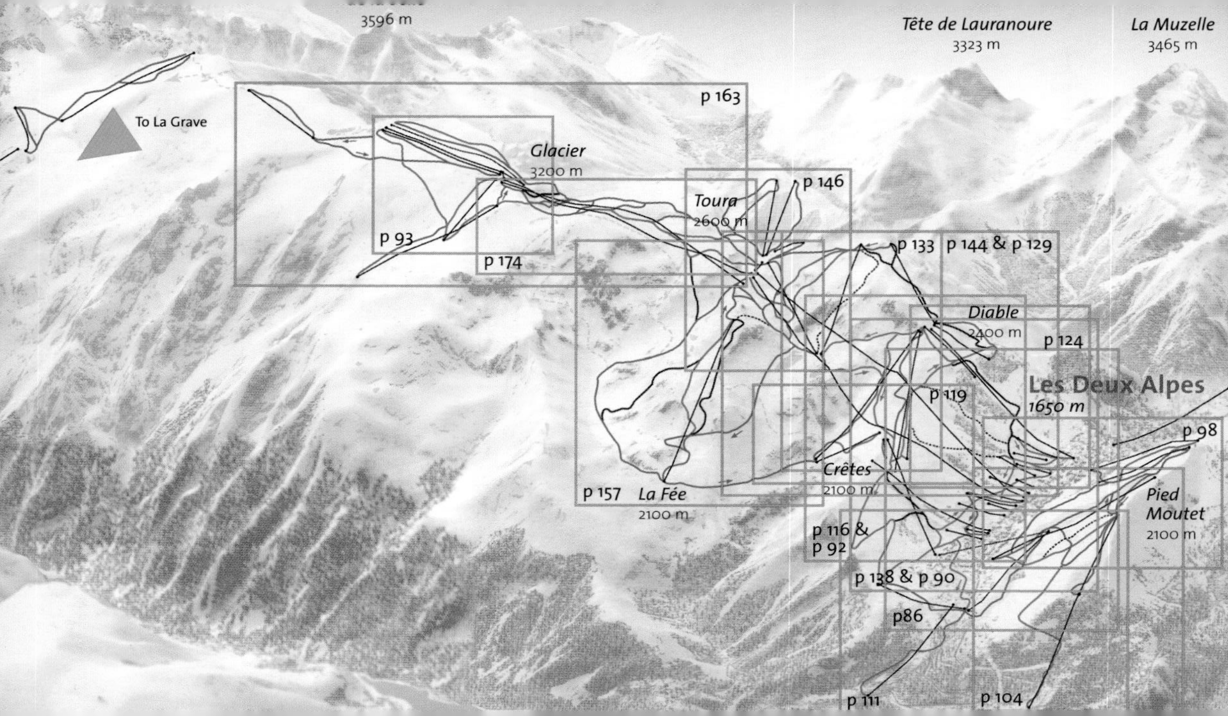
3596 m
Tête de Lauranoure
3323 m
La Muzelle
3465 m
To La Grave
p 163
Glacier
3200 m
p 93
p 174
Toura
2600 m
p 146
p 133
p 144 & p 129
Diable
2400 m
p 124
Les Deux Alpes
1650 m
p 119
p 98
p 157
La Fée
2100 m
Crêtes
2100 m
Pied
Moutet
2100 m
p 116 &
p 92
p 138 & p 90
p86
p 111
p 104

SKI PASSES

Various options are available, depending on duration and on whether you want a local or a full area pass. Prices are consistent throughout the main season, with no high season supplements.

A photograph is required for all passes of more than five day's duration: the passes are not electronically readable and must be displayed at all times. Lost passes will not be replaced or refunded.

LOCAL AND AREA PASS OPTIONS

Bas de Pistes A local pass covering all draglifts on the lowest town slopes only; available on a daily basis.

Ski Sympa A local pass covering all low- and mid-altitude lifts (lifts numbered 1–21 inclusive); available on a daily basis.

Super Ski Full area pass, covering all lifts; available as day passes and multiples thereof – the longer the duration, the cheaper the equivalent daily rate; also available as a 'Smart Pass' of five daily passes which can be used on any five non-consecutive days throughout the season.

Access to the nearby lifts and off-piste ski area at La Grave is available at a supplement on all Super Ski passes of up to five day's duration; passes of at least six day's duration automatically include this access at no additional cost (subject to the links being open), as well as access to Alpe d'Huez and the Grande Galaxie ski region (see pages 71 and 72).

All Super Ski passes of more than six days duration additionally include free access to Les Deux Alpes' ice rink (small charge for skate hire) and outdoor heated swimming pool; special discounts are also offered on a range of alternative activities for holders of these passes – for current terms and conditions, enquire at the central ski pass sales office in place des 2 Alpes.

SPECIAL OFFERS & DISCOUNTS

All full area passes are available for children (5–12 years), adults (13–59 years) and seniors (60–71 years); local passes are available at a set rate and on a daily basis only.

Ski passes are free of charge for all children under 5 years of age; 5–12 years of age prices for full area passes are approximately 25 per cent cheaper than adults. Full area ski passes for guests aged from 60–71 years of age are also approximately 25 per cent cheaper than standard adult passes; ski passes are free for the over 72s. Child/senior discounts are available for full-area ('Super Ski') passes only.

Part day From first lift to 13.00 hours; from 11.30 hours to lifts closing time; or, from 13.30 hours until lifts closing time.
Large families Special rates are available for larger families with a minimum of three children under 18 years of age; applies when purchasing a minimum of three weekly ski passes; available from the central ski pass sales office in place des 2 Alpes.
Last minute After 16.00 hours, a single one-way pedestrian-rate pass is available to squeeze in the longest run you can manage (use the Jandri Express cable car, lift number 55); handy on your first day if you arrive in resort before the lifts close.
Early season Ten per cent discount is given on all weekly ski passes during the first few weeks of the season; available from the station's opening date until the weekend before Christmas.
Full season Covering the entire season in Les Deux Alpes plus unlimited access to La Grave and Alpe d'Huez.

ⓘ Proof of age/identity is required at the time of purchase for all child, senior and family ski passes.

SKI PASS SALES POINTS

All passes are available from four main sales offices (see town plan on pages 63 ad 65). Additionally, you can purchase any of the day passes offered at any of the ski pass sales kiosks located at the base of a number of ski lifts dotted around the main resort. All family and full season ski passes are only available from the central ski pass office in the place des 2 Alpes.

MAIN SALES OFFICES

Place des 2 Alpes (Central ski pass office)
Grande Place, Les 2 Alpes 1800 quarter
Place de Mont-de-Lans, Alpe de Mont-de-Lans quarter
Place de Venosc, Alpe de Venosc quarter

DAY PASS SALES KIOSKS

At the following lift bases:
Petite Aiguille chair lift (2)
Viking button lift (13)
Venosc-Village gondola lift (17)
Super Venosc chair lift (21)
Belle Étoile chair lift (26)

NORDIC SKIING

Les Deux Alpes has just two short Nordic circuits (see page 190), both are easily accessible on foot from the main resort; no ski pass is required to use them and access is free-of-charge for all responsible users. You will of course need to purchase a pedestrian pass if you want to use any of the ski lifts from the satellite villages. A further attractive itinerary is also available down in the Vénéon valley near Venosc.

FREE LIFTS

Four button lifts on Les Deux Alpes' town slopes are free-of-charge and open to all responsible users, without the need for a ski pass, these are: Petit Bosquet (5), Coolidge Nord (10), Coolidge Sud (11) and the Petit Viking (13).

The gentle green pistes running down parallel to these lifts provide beginners and nervous novices with the opportunity to find their ski legs before purchasing a lift pass.

GRANDE GALAXIE SKI REGION

All Super Ski passes of at least six days duration include access to all ski stations in the Grande Galaxie ski region: covering two days skiing in the Grandes Rousses ski domain (Alpe d'Huez, Villard Reculas, Auris-en-Oisans, Oz-en-Oisans and Vaujany), as well as one free-of-charge day-pass for Puy-St-Vincent, Serre Chevalier or the Milky Way domain straddling the French/Italian border. Visits to these stations must be made during the period of validity of your Les Deux Alpes Super ski pass. Transport is not included (see page 72 for details of the shuttle service to Alpe d'Huez).

! Accident insurance is not included in basic ski pass prices, so make sure you are adequately covered or take the insurance supplement offered. Never take to the slopes without comprehensive winter sports travel insurance (see page 52).

PRICES

For current prices of all ski passes, tuition and childcare, please go to our website: **www.ski-ride.com**

ALPE D'HUEZ SHUTTLE

Since all Super Ski ski passes of minimum six days duration include two days skiing at nearby Alpe d'Huez and the linked Grandes Rousses ski domain, a special shuttle bus service operates from Les Deux Alpes twice per week (currently Wednesday and Thursday). The service runs from/to the central bus station at the place des 2 Alpes and the bus stop at the place de Mont-de-Lans roundabout. The bus currently departs Les Deux Alpes at 08.30 hours, arriving in Alpe d'Huez around 09.45 hours; leaving Alpe d'Huez for the return journey at 17.20 hours and arriving back into Les Deux Alpes around 18.35 hours. The service operates from the last week in December to the last week in April, subject to road conditions and demand; ticket prices are excellent value, currently in single figures for the two-way trip. Places are limited and must be booked 48 hours in advance: bookings may be made directly at the main VFD office at 112 avenue de la Muzelle and at the branch office at the tourist office annex on the roundabout at place de Mont-de-Lans. Central booking, contact: ⓣ +33 (0)4 76 80 51 22 ⓦ www.vdf.fr

Bergers area at Alpe d'Huez towards Pic Blanc

SKI BUS

There are three lines operated by the ski bus (navette) service in Les Deux Alpes, all colour-coded specific to the areas they serve. The service is free of charge for all visitors and no ski pass is required to use the service.

⊖ **Red Line** (Circuit Rouge): running in a circuit around the entire central resort from/to the place de Mont-de-Lans roundabout at the resort entrance » avenue de la Muzelle » rue des Vikings » rue des Sagnes » avenue de la Muzelle; approximately every 10 minutes from 08.00–20.00 hours.

⊖ **Green Line** (Circuit Vert): running in a circuit around l'Alpe de Venosc quarter via the place de la Croix des Limites » rue du Rouchas » rue du Cairou » avenue de la Muzelle » rue des Vikings; approximately every 15 minutes from 08.00–20.00 hours.

⊖ **Blue Line** (Circuit Bleu): serving the lower l'Alpe de Mont-de-Lans end of the resort and Les 2 Alpes 1800 quarter, running in a circuit from/to the place de Mont-de-Lans roundabout » route de Champamé » place des Arcades » route du Petit Plan » the lower end of avenue de la Muzelle; approximately every 15 minutes from 08.00–20.00 hours.

Timetables are posted on 25 bus stops dotted around the resort and are also available from the tourist offices; times are subject to road conditions and passenger numbers. A combined routes service operates at a reduced frequency during the weeks leading up to Christmas.

EQUIPMENT

Most visitors travelling with a tour operator tend to leave the organisation of equipment to their Reps; newly arrived guests will then usually be taken en masse for gear fitting on their first morning before going on the mountain.

Virtually every sports shop in Les Deux Alpes offers a snowsports equipment rental operation, so there's plenty of choice and competition to keep standards high and prices keen. All of the major franchises are represented, including Sport2000 and Twinner, InterSport and SkiSet plus there are a number of independent businesses providing bespoke services, including latest models hire. As the station focuses so heavily on newschool snowsports, there are a good number of freestyle, snowboard and back-country equipment specialists. You can try:

SkiSet at Slide Planet ⓐ 82 avenue de la Muzelle (opposite the place des 2 Alpes) ⓣ +33 (0)4 76 79 04 71 ⓦ www.slideplanet.com

Reservoir Boards ⓐ galerie l'Arlequin, 61–69 avenue de la Muzelle ⓣ +33 (0)4 76 11 36 88

Sliders Surf Shop ⓐ 4 galerie la Sénéou, 61 avenue de la Muzelle ⓣ +33 (0)4 76 79 09 15

Atelier du Snowboard ⓐ place des Arcades, Les 2 Alpes 1800 ⓣ +33 (0)4 76 79 01 73 ⓦ www.snowboard-atelier.com

TUITION

There's no shortage of choice when it comes to ski schools and courses available, with everything from standard group lessons for absolute beginners and progressing novices up to advanced one-to-one teaching clinics for advanced level all-mountain riders, for both ski and snowboard. Children generally need to be at least three years old before they are accepted into ski school.

The big national ski school operation, **l'École du Ski Français** (ESF), has a number of offices in Les Deux Alpes. ESF central information office: t +33 (0)4 76 79 21 21 w www.esf2alpes.com

There are also a number of specialised independent ski schools, the following are some of the best:
European Ski School With native British (or advanced English-speaking) instructors and a maximum group size of four persons. Video analysis. Courses available – all levels, children and adults; snowboard, freeride, off-piste and carving. a Based at the Hotel le Crêt, 95 avenue de la Muzelle t +33 (0)4 76 79 74 55 w www.europeanskischool.co.uk

St-Christophe International Ski & Snowboard School Part of the ESI network; group and private lessons; specialist children's tuition and childcare; newschool snowsports, carving, blading and Telemark. a avenue de la Muzelle t +33 (0)4 76 79 04 21 w www.oisans.com/ecoleski.2alpes

Burton Connexion Specialist snowboard tuition as part of the Burton Snowboards worldwide 'Learn to Ride' programme. Group size maximum four persons and international guest instructors; courses for all levels. a Hameau du Courtil, Venosc t +33 (0)6 15 07 94 42 w www.oisans.com/burtonconnexion

Stages Ski Freeride Damien Albert Specialist freeride, off-piste and bumps tuition; video analysis; maximum group size eight persons; available to competent black run skiers only.
a Based at the Hotel Chalet Mounier, 2 rue de la Chapelle
t +33 (0)4 76 79 50 38 w www.abc-skifreeride.com

For more experienced visitors, Les Deux Alpes **Bureau des Guides** is also an excellent option. The team of high mountain guides are, unlike standard ski instructors, qualified to guide on the off-piste glacier routes; they also offer heliskiing, search and rescue training, ice climbing, Via Ferrata rock climbing, snow-shoeing and ski touring to other regional ski stations. The Bureau des Guides information and booking office is based at the Maison des 2 Alpes. ⓐ place des 2 Alpes ⓣ +33 (0)4 76 11 36 29

NON-SKIERS

Les Deux Alpes has a good selection of sports and leisure activities and facilities; it also has an extensive network of ski lifts accessible to pedestrians, allowing non-skiers to access most high-altitude restaurants and viewpoints. Pedestrian passes are available for four different altitude zones – the higher you want to go, the higher the price; full area (all zones) pedestrian passes permit travel on a total of 13 ski lifts: including all major gondolas and cable cars, the funicular on the glacier plus some chairlifts. A dedicated walkers guide and panoramic peak identifier is published and is available from all tourist offices and ski pass sales points.

SNOW GARDENS & CHILDCARE

There are three gentle, fenced-off Snow Gardens especially for children on the main town slopes; one near the Vikings button lift (13), one in front of the Jandri lifts base stations (25 and 55) and one near the Champamé button lift (3). All are close to the resort and its services and are easy to reach on foot. The sites are equipped with gentle rope tows and colourful easy obstacles; they are controlled by the ESF and St-Christophe International ski school

Welcome to the wonderful world of snowsports

(see page 75 for contact details), both of which have specialist nursery ski instructors available to introduce children aged over 3 years to the world of snowsports; lift passes are required to use these facilities, but these are free for all children under 5 years old. Available half-days, full-days and weekly.

Additionally, most ski schools also offer standard skiing lessons out in the main beginners' areas for children aged over 6 years of age. Prices are generally around 20 per cent cheaper than those for adult classes.

PREPARATION

Please ensure that your children are equipped with the correct technical clothing, gloves, hat, proper sunglasses or goggles, sun protection lotion and handkerchiefs. Helmets are also strongly recommended.

It is a good idea to pack some snacks for them too, and to put your contact details in their pocket.

Crèche Les 2 Alpes 1800 Dedicated creche for children aged 6 months–2 years old. The crèche is modern and well equipped and has a quiet zone for sleepy heads. The service must be booked at least one day in advance and is available on a half-day or full-day basis, meals can also be provided; 08.30–17.30 hours. Children are supervised by a qualified nursery team and take part in a variety of leisure and learning activities. ⓐ Hameau du Lautaret, Les 2 Alpes 1800 ⓣ +33 (0)4 76 79 02 62

Le Bonhomme de Neige Day-care and activities centre for children aged 2–6 and 6–12 years old. Enrolment is pre-bookable or available on the spot, subject to demand; available on a half-day or full-day basis, meals can also be provided. Children are supervised by a qualified nursery team and participate in a wide range of leisure and educational activities, including arts and crafts, music and cookery. Children must arrive before 10.00 hours and be picked up before 15.00 hours. ⓐ rue de Sagnes (central Les Deux Alpes) ⓣ +33 (0)4 76 79 06 77

ⓘ Adaption period – crèche and daycare centres normally ask that you enrol your children for half-days only for the first two days. This is to allow children time to settle in.

VACCINATIONS & MEDICAL RECORDS

Resort childcare services may ask for proof that your child has had certain vaccinations. You are advised to contact them well in advance of your trip to ascertain exact requirements.

SERVICES

Medical Centres There are well-equipped trauma and X-ray suites available at two separate medical centres in Les Deux Alpes: one in the town centre on avenue de la Muzelle and one on the rue des Vikings in the Alpe de Venosc quarter, near the Diable gondola-lift base station (23) and directly accessible from the pistes (see town plans on pages 63 and 65).

Centre Clinique des 2 Alpes ⓐ 80 avenue de la Muzelle
ⓣ +33 (0)4 76 79 20 03
Centre Médical du Lauvitel ⓐ 3 rue des Vikings
ⓣ +33 (0)4 76 80 52 48

The medical staff will contact your insurance company, however you will have to pay any initial costs, excluded by any excess clauses, on-site. Make sure that your insurance covers heli-rescue, piste rescue and ambulance transport as well as medical and hospital expenses.

ⓘ Always carry ID and your insurance details. It is also advisable to carry a small first-aid kit for dealing with minor cuts and bruises (see Health & Safety, pages 47–52).

Telephones Phonecard and coin-operated public telephone booths are plentiful around Les Deux Alpes town; once out on the slopes there are public telephones sited at the largest mountain restaurants. There are also a couple of public telephone booths in the villages of Mont-de-Lans and Venosc. Phonecards are available from tobacconists and most convenience stores and souvenir shops. GSM mobile phone coverage is virtually 100 per cent within the ski domain boundaries.

WCs Off the slopes, these are situated at the Venosc gondola lift base station; beside the tourist office annex at place de l'Alpe de Venosc; at the central tourist office in place des 2 Alpes, on the avenue de la Muzelle in the resort centre; at the tourist office annex on the roundabout at place de Mont-de-Lans; and at the Grand Place in Les Deux Alpes 1800 quarter. On the mountain, there are public WCs at the top of the Super Venosc chair lift (21) in the Pied Moutet sector; at the rear of the Chalet Toura restaurant at the Toura 2600 interchange area and at the large piste-patrol building in the middle of the Glacier 3200 interchange area. All of the mountain restaurants also have public toilets; some of these are serviced and levy a small charge.

ATMs There are over half a dozen cash machines dotted along the arterial avenue de la Muzelle. The closest to the town slopes is at the Crédit Agricole bank on avenue de la Muzelle, near the central place des 2 Alpes. The closest to the Pied Moutet sector slopes is at the Banque Populaire des Alpes, near the place de Mont-de-Lans (see town plans on pages 63 and 65). Instructions in English are easy to find and operation similar to those in your own bank.

Mountain restaurants There are seven different sites at various altitudes throughout the ski area, all of which are directly accessible by ski lift and/or piste. Most are attractive, atmospheric venues offering good quality à la carte fare; all offer a full bar service and most have snack food options too. Three are self-service.

There are also plenty of venues spread along the edge of the central town slopes and at the Grande Place in Les Deux Alpes 1800, again all easily accessible from the pistes.

➔ *See page 181 for specific restaurant reviews.*

Picnic areas Les Deux Alpes has lots of designated outdoor picnic spots spread throughout the ski domain, many at spectacular viewpoints. There are always a few benches and tables provided, along with rubbish bins The sites are marked on the local piste map with a little 'P' symbol. It is forbidden to picnic on any of the restaurant terraces.

There are two indoor picnic saloons. These are very plain and quite bare, simply furnished with some tables, chairs and with bins provided. However, they are both sheltered, fairly bright with plenty of natural daylight and are close to other services:

- Tucked underneath the terrace at La Patache restaurant at the Crêtes 2100 interchange area
- On the ground floor of the Jandri Express 2 cable car upper station at the Glacier 3200 interchange area

Please help protect this beautiful environment by putting all your rubbish, plus any that you find, in a bin.

Le Panoramic mountain restaurant terrace, Toura 2600

SNOWFALL HISTORY & ANALYSIS

Although precipitation is unpredictable at very long range, patterns do emerge that are observable over a number of seasons. Using this data, you can tell if your preferred period of travel has historically seen good snow cover. The magic figure is 100 cm (39 in) – once snow depth exceeds this mark, conditions are generally good throughout the ski area and will remain so for a more extended period.

Since Les Deux Alpes boasts Europe's largest skiable glacier, snow quantity and quality on the upper slopes is almost guaranteed. The season usually gets underway in November and extends to the end of April. The glacier is open from mid-June to late August for summer skiing, too. All principal town slopes are covered by snowmaking equipment, as are the link routes to/from the Pied Moutet sector. The only negative issue is that the lower slopes often become very heavy and slushy in warm weather.

The chart below details combined averages recorded over three seasons immediately before the publication of this guide. Visit **www.ski-ride.com** for live snow reports.

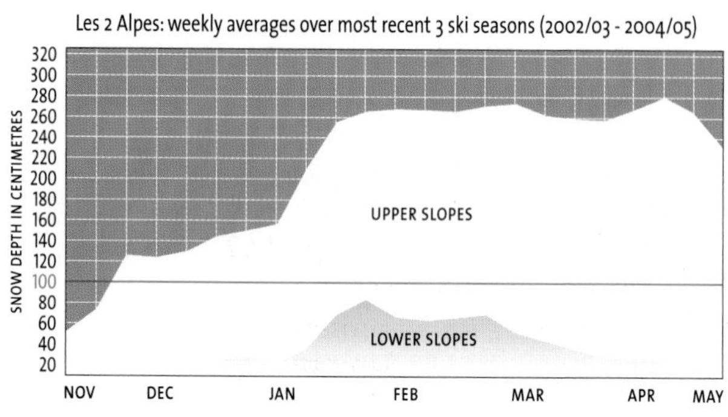

PREVIOUS SEASONS' SNOWFALL BREAKDOWN BY YEAR

The following charts detail the snowfall history for the three most recent seasons. Data from these charts was used to compile the combined averages chart on the preceding page.

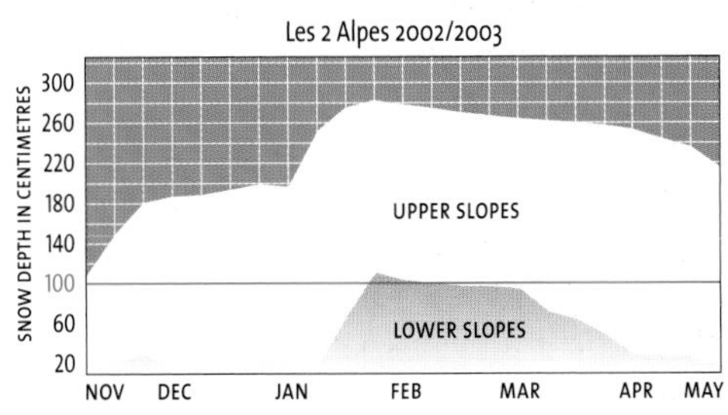

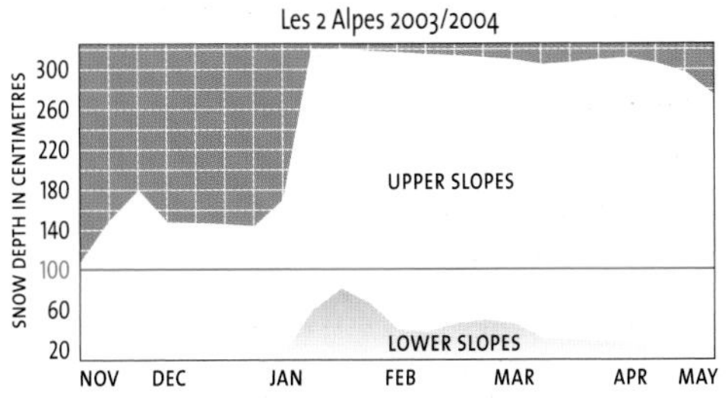

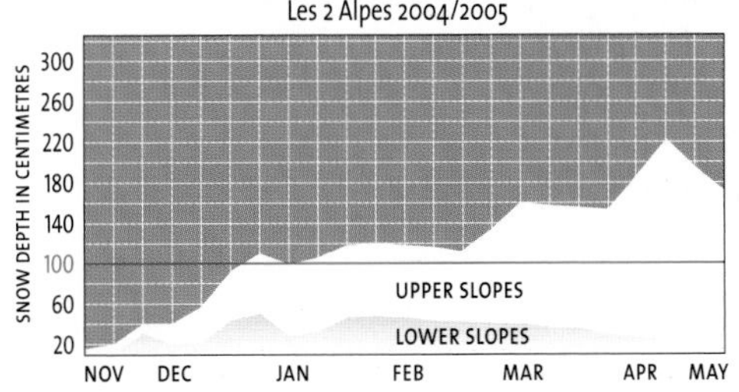

ESF
ADULTE

LES DEUX ALPES BASE

Because Les Deux Alpes stretches out in a linear fashion along the flat floor of a long col, its town slopes also sprawl along the lowest flanks of the mountains which rise up either side. This means that no matter where you are staying in the main resort, you are never more than a short stroll from the pistes.

The central town slopes, spreading out from behind the main tourist information and ski pass offices at place des 2 Alpes, serve as the principal base focus: as a departure point for the main lifts to the core ski area; for ski school classes and for children discovering the joys of snowsports on the gentle wide lower pistes and Snow Gardens; for weekend dabblers availing of the free-of-charge button lifts; and for non-skiers and locals simply relaxing alongside snowsports enthusiasts, sipping an aperitif, sun-bathing and seeing-and-being-seen at the street-level piste-side bars and restaurants, or skating or driving bumper cars on the ice rink (see page 191) or swimming in the outdoor heated pool (see page 194).

FIRST ACCESS

On the eastern side of Les Deux Alpes, columns of ski lifts rise perpendicular to the line of the town, from various points almost all the way from one end of the resort to the other: a total of 18 running side-by-side, 14 of which serve the almost completely pisted and lightly wooded hillside covered by the town slopes.

You can wander on to the pistes from various points along the main arterial roads, but the principal access points for the core ski area are at the place des 2 Alpes and the rue des Vikings (see town plans on pages 63 and 65).

Main ski school meeting points on the central town slopes

The main uplift to the core ski area is provided by the Jandri Express 1 cable car (55) (see page 143), housed in a huge base station at the bottom of the central town slopes, carrying passengers directly to the Toura 2600 area interchange and connecting with the Jandri Express 2 cable car for the onward access to the glacial zones at 3200 m (10,496 ft). Next to the Jandri Express 1 is an equally large base station for the Jandri 1 gondola lift (25) (see page 117), which rises to the Crêtes 2100 area interchange and connects with the Jandri 2 cable car for the onward journey to Toura 2600. Both base stations, and the surrounding services and facilities, are easy to reach from the town slopes, centred on the Lutins blue piste which is served by a button lift of the same name (lift no. 8).

A number of traverse tracks cut diagonally across the top and middle of the town slopes in both directions, with just enough slope angle to allow a gentle on-piste glide from one end of resort to the other, meaning you can take any of the shorter lower lifts to gain height and then make a cross-hill link to most of the other lifts. All of these routes are accurately graded green or blue and the entire town slopes area is accessible to visitors of all abilities.

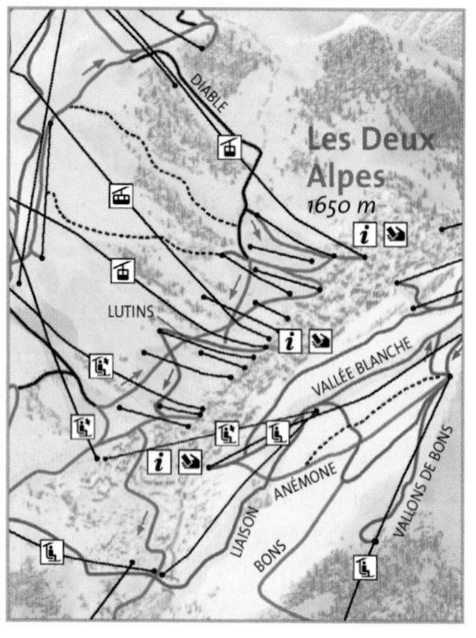

Those staying at the northern Alpe de Mont-de-Lans quarter also have the option of taking the Belle Étoile chair lift (26) (see page 116), reachable from the roadside from the route de Champamé and from the top of the rue du Grand Plan, to link with the Crêtes 2100 area interchange; this is a 2-way lift, so novices, early intermediates and pedestrians can use it to return to base again, otherwise, they can use the Chemin des Demoiselles green route (see page 141); more advanced ability visitors can also return to this base area via the Valentin black piste (see page 140).

The southern Alpe de Venosc quarter houses another major lift, the Diable gondola lift (23) (see page 124), rising to the Diable 2400 area interchange. The Diable's base station is located on the rue des Vikings; a pisted track is maintained from the town slopes down to the roadside, finishing just a few metres from the station building to ensure ease of access for those already on the slopes. The steep upper flanks of the mountain directly above the town slopes are furrowed with wooded gullies, the only home runs tracing down them being fairly testing black runs, half of them ungroomed; novices and early intermediates either have to return to resort using the main lifts or descend on-piste using the long Chemin des Demoiselles green (see page 141).

QUEUE JUMP TO CRÊTES 2100

The Jandri and Diable ski lifts are usually very busy first thing every morning. A good queue jump is to head to the Belle Étoile chair lift (26) (see page 116) then take the Ancontres button lift (30) to reach the Crêtes 2100 interchange (see page 118).

LES 2 ALPES 1800

This purpose-built satellite accommodation zone (also known as 'le Village') is perched 150 m (492 ft) above the Alpe de Mont-de-Lans quarter; it has its own compact base area focused around the buzzing Grande Place commercial plaza, at the uppermost and most northerly margins of Les Deux Alpes. This plaza houses a fair number of lively bars and restaurants, a decent-sized supermarket for picnic provisions; plus a tourist office annex and a ski pass sales point. The Village chair lift (27) (see page 115) is the sole lift rising from this area, connecting with the key Crêtes 2100 area interchange for all onward links to the core ski domain. The chair lift and the Grande Place are reachable on-piste via the Chemin des Demoiselles green route and the Valentin black piste; the former also continuing past this level to complete the traverse towards the main town slopes and base areas, as well as giving access to a pisted link route through the residential area down to the base of La Cote chair lift to link with the Pied Moutet sector.

FIRST DAY

Equipment rental is best organized either first thing after arriving in resort or early on your first morning before going on to the slopes. If you are travelling with a tour operator, your rep will handle logistics and take you for equipment fitting en masse with other newly arrived guests.

If booked into ski school, you will then be advised where to meet, or accompanied to whichever rendevous area is nearest to you accommodation; ski school generally begins around 10.00 hours.

PIED MOUTET

The separate Pied Moutet sector rises more steeply above the western side of Les Deux Alpes, with just two lifts accessible from street level: the Vallée Blanche chair lift (19) (see page 102) by the Mont-de-Lans roundabout; and the Super Venosc chair lift (21) (see page 97) just above the rue du Rouchas in the Alpe de Venosc quarter, reached by a long flight of steps from the arterial avenue de la Muzelle.

Home run pistes flow back to the base of both lifts, but there are no real town slopes to speak of and the whole sector is much quieter than the principal base areas on the other side of town.

OTHER ACCESS POINTS

The Venosc gondola lift (17) (07.45–19.00 daily, 7½ minutes journey time) rises from the roadside in the Vénéon valley, near the village of Venosc, to an upper station at the bottom end of the rue Sainte Luce in the Alpe de Venosc quarter of Les Deux Alpes; from there you will need to walk around 250 m (274 yd) further to reach the nearest ski lift, which is the Diable gondola lift (23).

From Mont-de-Lans village, the old Mont-de-Lans chair lift (1) (see page 112) rises from the main roadside at the upper end of the village, above a home-run red piste of the same name, arriving within easy on-piste reach of the Petite Aiguille chair lift (2) (see page 113) and connecting with the Chemin des Demoiselles green route for all onward options as described for Les 2 Alpes 1800.

There is a car park near the base of the Petite Aiguille chair lift; this area can be reached on-piste from the Pied Moutet sector via a pisted foot bridge across the D213 road, and a new 4-person chair lift (La Cote) will be opened here during the 2006 season to make the link in the opposite direction.

BEGINNERS' ZONES

Like many ski stations, Les Deux Alpes has beginners' zones on the gentlest slopes immediately next to the resort, but it is unusual for also having substantial beginners' pistes at the uppermost reaches of the ski domain, on the glacier above 3200 m (10,496 ft); allowing beginners to share in the incredible buzz of super-high-altitude skiing, with stunning Alpine panoramas as a bonus.

The Crêtes 2100 area interchange at 2100 m (6888 ft), at the top of the first major lifts out of town, also houses a sizable beginners' zone and, like the town slopes, is much more sheltered and familiar than the exposed and dizzying heights of the glacial zone. All of the beginners' zones are within each reach of major lifts and services, the town slopes naturally being very handy for all resort facilities too.

TOWN SLOPES

The principal ESF ski school meeting points run along the base of the pistes next to the Jandri Express 1 cable car base station, easily accessible from the upper right-hand corner of the place des 2 Alpes in the centre of the resort, just beyond the central ski pass office and handy for L'Orée des Pistes button lift (9) and the free-of-charge Coolidge Nord and Sud button lifts (10 and 11).

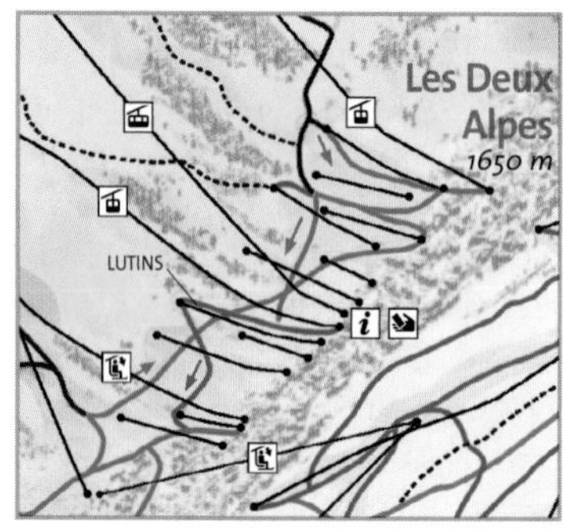

The area immediately in front of the hotel Les Melezes, in the middle of the rue des Vikings, is also easily accessible from the roadside and the pistes, and houses the Vikings (13) and Grand Viking (14) button lifts, the former being one of the resort's free-of-charge ski lifts. These serve the gentle slopes next to further ski school meeting points and are handy for all users to gain height from this end of the resort to glide over to the central meeting points and principal lifts, or to do the same in the opposite direction to reach the more progressive and longer green pistes at the southern-most end of the town slopes, which are served by the Gentianes and Rivets button lifts (15 and 16).

At the Mont-de-Lans quarter, the ski school meeting points are around the base of the Belle Étoile chair lift (26), next to the Petit Bosquet, Bosquet and Champamé button lifts (5, 4 and 3 respectively). Between here and the central town slopes there are slightly quieter slopes served by l'Alpette chair lift (6), which is the sole chair lift serving the beginners' zones, and the Limaçons and Lutins button lifts (7 and 8).

All of the lowest altitude town slopes are groomed to form motorway-wide superpistes. They are all designated as a beginners' zone, in one continuous strip along the resort, clearly signed as such on the pistes to instruct all users travelling through these zones to limit their speed. Most are gentle, easy green pistes which are accurately graded, however, the blue pistes served by the Lutins button lift (8) and the Côte Brune button lift (12) are actually quite steep and provide progressing beginners with a real first challenge once they have got to grips with the basics.

The main children's Snow Garden is safely fenced off from the main pistes on the slopes in front of the Jandri 1 gondola lift base station, with additional sites near the Belle Étoile chair lift (26) and near the rue des Vikings lifts. All are within easy reach of the resort and services and are equipped with simple rope tows and/or magic carpet conveyor-belt lifts, plus colourful cartoon character display boards and fun obstacles. These facilities are monitored by specialist nursery instructors from the ESF and St Christophe International Ski School and are subject to demand – pre-booking recommended (see page 75 for contact details).

CRÊTES 2100 AREA

Although this area looks quite compact on the piste map, it actually has a fairly substantial beginners' zone, fanning out over a wide open area close to La Patache bar/restaurant; easily accessible from town using the Jandri 1 gondola lift (25) or the Belle Étoile chair lift (26). The area is directly above Les Deux Alpes and has good views over the town and towards the Pied Moutet sector on the opposite side of the valley.

The designated beginners' zones share the slopes with the Crêtes blue and Petites Crêtes green pistes (see Crêtes blue description on page 122), segregated from them by ropes and traffic-control netting. These slopes are a central focus for the ski schools at the end of the week, when they organize beginners' and novices' races, present certificates and award badges.

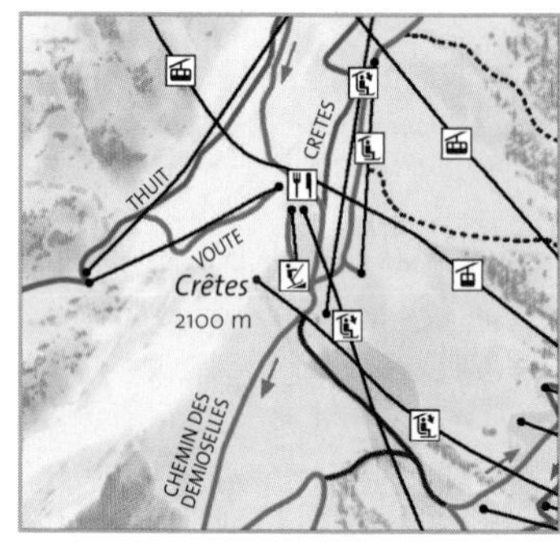

A couple of chair lifts and short rope tows serve the Crêtes 2100 area pistes themselves (see page 118 for orientation); the Crêtes chair lift (28) (see page 122) and the Jandri 2 cable car (33) (see page 144) also leave this major interchange area to facilitate first forays out into the core ski area.

To return to Les Deux Alpes, beginners can either take the long, flat and often patchy Chemin des Demoiselles green route all the way down to the town slopes, or simply ride back down on one of the main two-way lifts.

GLACIER 3200 AREA

An amazing experience for first-time visitors to the high Alps, providing a real buzz of sharing the glacial summits with experienced snowsports enthusiasts and mountaineers, and on clear days offering a spectacular vantage point to take in the vistas over the major Alpine summits extending into Italy and Switzerland.

Absolute beginners will start out on the principal beginners' zone at Les Deux Alpes town slopes, before being brought up to this altitude after the first couple of days of getting to grips with unfamiliar equipment. This area is best accessed using the linked Jandri Express 1 and 2 cable cars (55 and 56) (see pages 143 and 161).

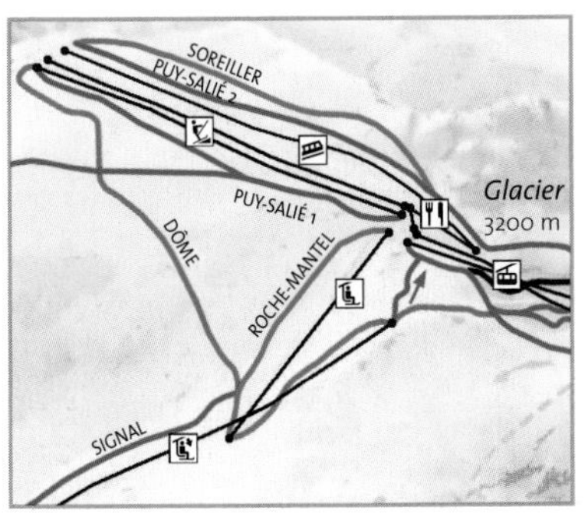

The main glacier area is served by the Dôme Express funicular (54) (see page 166) and a number of T-bar lifts; the former is an underground tube train, a fantastic piece of engineering burrowing through the bedrock towards the summit; accessible by skiers and non-skiers. This area is where the extensive summer-ski snow park is located during July and August and it is a popular year-round point of interest for all visitors, drawn by the nearby Grotte de Glace (ice cave – see page 189) and viewpoint orientation table.

The beginners' zone at this altitude is centred on the Soreiller green piste, at the gentlest southern edge of the wide and well-groomed ice flow; parallel to this are the Puy Salié 1 and 2 T-bars (47 and 48) (see page 167) flanked by two busier namesake blue pistes; handy for progression out on to the main pistes once the beginners' zone is conquered. All these slopes flow down to a huge restaurant and services structure at the major Glacier 3200 area interchange (see page 163 for orientation).

Competent novices can ski all the way back to resort from this altitude, but the easiest way is to descend using the cable car.

CAUTION

You are now on a glacier, where dangerous crevasses are numerous even if you can't see them. The piste patrol have clearly marked out the pistes and safe footpaths – you are strongly advised to stay on them.

If you take off your skis or board, you become simply an un-roped pedestrian in a serious mountaineering environment, so keep your gear on at all times when moving around on the glacial pistes.

In safe hands – the younger you start the easier it is

PIED MOUTET SECTOR

This is a completely distinct sector on the western side of Les Deux Alpes, spread over a single compact hillside with just the one circuitous on-piste link to the core ski area on the opposite side of town. The entire sector can be skied-out in less than a day, but it does have the advantage of being much quieter than the other sectors and the whole hillside can be ridden to deliver a respectable variety of terrain. The enjoyable cruises on the attractive wooded slopes down to Mont-de-Lans and Bons also have the novelty factor of reaching the lowest skiable points in the domain. Main access is via two roadside chair lifts, one at either end of town.

SUPER VENOSC CHAIR LIFT (21)

- 431 m (1414 ft) vertical rise
- 1285 m (1406 yd) long
- 1200 passengers/hour

Located just above the rue du Rouchas, at the Venosc end of Les Deux Alpes, reached by a long flight of steps from the avenue de la Muzelle. There is a ski pass kiosk at the get-on point, although this sells day passes only.

At the top of the lift, turn right on to the wide, flat ridge. The lift operator's structure houses public eco-WCs. The Troïka bar/restaurant (see page 182) is on the higher ground above right. U-turn to the right down the lift line to begin the Super Venosc red, or follow the wide traverse across the upper slopes above the nearby piste-patrol hut for all other pistes. An off-piste itinerary down to the hamlet of Les Travers begins over the boundary fence ahead (see page 100).

Troïka restaurant terraces towards the peak of La Muzelle

ORIENTATION

The Pied Moutet ridge marks the westernmost limit of the patrolled ski area. The Troïka bar/restaurant (see page 182) occupies the highest ground – on a clear day it is a great vantage point to orientate yourself within the ski domain. The Super Venosc chair lift (21) arrives just in front of the Troïka; the imposing pyramidal peak on the skyline beyond is the Aiguille de Venosc, with La Muzelle just behind it to the left. Both summits are at the far side of the Vénéon Valley, above the lift-linked village of Venosc, at the edge of the Ecrins National Park.

Turning left, you are looking over Les Deux Alpes town and towards the core ski area on the mountainside opposite. All major lifts are visible rising from the far side of town, with the home run pistes pouring down the slopes beneath them. The lift arriving behind the Troïka is the Pied Moutet chair lift (20); the wide pisted traverse running off to the left (signed as the 'Liaison Vallée Blanche') under this lift line and across the upper slopes provides access to the rest of the Pied Moutet sector.

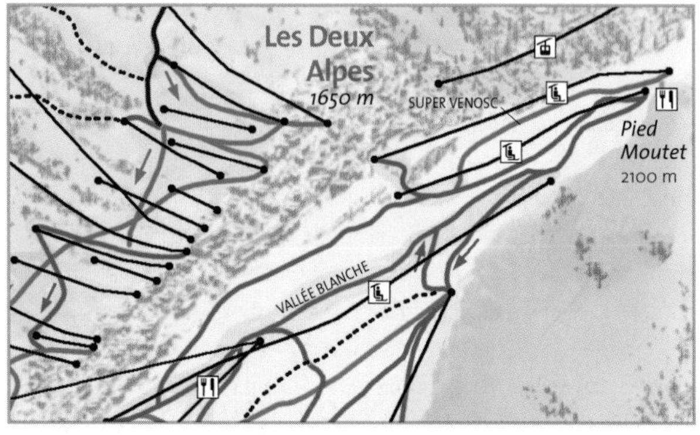

SUPER VENOSC

Not long, but a good warm-up run, with great views over the Vénéon Valley and across Les Deux Alpes to the core ski area. From the wide shared start area on the ridge, stick to the right past the piste-patrol cabin and descend parallel to the line of the Super Venosc chair lift (21). This wide upper section is really blue in profile, with a very flat mid-section ahead – so keep your momentum up. The piste veers closer to the lift line and then spills off the hillside on to steeper and more exciting terrain, with lots of lumps and bumps to get your legs working; the left-hand side of the piste delivers the steepest line. The mellower lower section sweeps left to make a good link with the nearby Pied Moutet chair lift (20) (see page 100), although there are also a couple of options to prolong the run. Hook to the right down into the tree line to join the lower section of the Pied Moutet blue piste for a fast cruise to the base of the Super Venosc chair lift (21) – the earlier you curve to the right, the steeper the descent remains; alternatively, simply glide past the get-on point for lift 20 to continue the long, gentle traverse across the lower slopes, out to the left to reach the base of the Vallée Blanche chair lift (19) which serves the rest of this sector.

Vénéon Valley viewed from the Super Venosc red

OFF-PISTE INITIATION

Beyond the ski-area boundary fence at the top of the Super Venosc chair lift (21) lies a wide, sparsely wooded valley which is ideal for a first off-piste tour.

The rocky upper section is fairly undemanding, over open and relatively gentle slopes. The lower section dips a little more steeply into the tree line and picks its way through well-spaced glades and offering some low-boulder drop-offs. The descent runs to the hamlet of Les Travers, a 15–20 minute hike along a quiet country road to the nearest ski lift at Bons. To discover this and other great off-piste routes in the area, always employ a qualified mountain guide (see page 76 for contact details).

PIED MOUTET CHAIR LIFT (20)

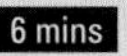

- 240 m (787 ft) vertical rise
- 855 m (935 yd) long
- 1100 passengers/hour

Mid-altitude location, reachable via the Super Venosc, Pied Moutet and Maïs pistes – useful when the lower slopes below this point are patchy and/or slushy. The pistes to the right below the lift on the journey up are the Pied Moutet blue (nearest) and the parallel Maïs red. The whole hillside under the lift line is open and provides good freeriding on powder days. On arrival at the top, there is a picnic spot ahead and the Troïka bar/restaurant is immediately to the left. U-turn to the left under the lift line to traverse to the start of the Pied Moutet blue, Maïs red, and Cimes and Vallée Blanche blues (good directional signage).

PIED MOUTET

From the ridge area beside the Troïka bar/restaurant, at the top of lifts 20 and 21, traverse across the upper slopes to run under the line of the Pied Moutet two-seater chair lift (20). There is a 20–30 m (22–33 yd) steepish pitch just before the Pied Moutet blue starts by dropping off down to the right. The upper section is motorway wide and maintains a steady gradient for its straight fall-line descent, parallel to the lift line, delivering a fast cruise and an opportunity to practise fast short turns. The Pied Moutet chair lift (20) is easily reached below right.

Alternatively, bypass the lift to continue the descent towards Les Deux Alpes town and to reach the other chair lifts serving this sector. Swinging to the left will take you on a long, gentle traverse to the Vallée Blanche chair lift (19) at the Monts-de-Lans end of town. Turning to the right continues as the Pied Moutet blue piste, sweeping across the hillside as a fast swath through the fir plantation, for a good link with the Super Venosc chair lift (21) at the Venosc end of town.

MAÏS

Slightly further out to the left of the Pied Moutet blue piste is the parallel course of the short Maïs red run. This mirrors the Pied Moutet but takes a steeper line, eventually swinging to the right to merge with its neighbour to reach the Pied Moutet chair lift (20). The steepest, deepest slopes to the sides of the piste are the biggest attraction of this route, offering enjoyable freeriding on powder days. To continue the descent to resort below chair lift 20, and/or to reach the other lifts serving this sector, follow the directions given for the Pied Moutet blue piste from that point.

VALLÉE BLANCHE CHAIR LIFT (19)

9 mins

- 419 m (1375 ft) vertical rise
- 1481 m (1620 yd) long
- 2600 passengers/hour

Located at the entrance to Les Deux Alpes, by the roadside beside the place de Monts-de-Lans roundabout and ski-bus stop, at the base of this sector's principal pistes. The get-on point is wide and flat and has a magic carpet to ease mounting.

The lift travels diagonally up the slopes, giving a bird's-eye view over most of the routes on this face of the mountain. On arrival at the top, dismount immediately next to the lift operator's hut (the final pylon is further on but there is quite a drop from the chair at that point); U-turn left for all pistes. There is an excellent information post with piste map, directional signs, clock and tool point on the piste junction below. Turn highest left under the arriving lift line for the Vallons de Bons blue traverse and to reach the Fioc black and the Anémone and Bons reds; or head to the right at the display board for the Maïs red and to cross to lifts 20 and 21; or simply head straight down for the Vallée Blanche and Cimes blues.

Studying options at the upper Vallée Blanche area

VALLÉE BLANCHE/CIMES

These two good blues begin together beside the central information post just below the arrival point of the Vallée Blanche chair lift (19). They are also accessible from any of the other lifts arriving on this ridge using the uppermost cross-mountain traverse routes (signed as 'liaison Vallée Blanche'). The Vallée Blanche is this sector's principal piste and is protected with snow-making from top to bottom; the Cimes is simply an easier variation. Their shared start area is wide and straightforward but has a respectably steep slope angle; furthest to the left, under the chair-lift line, the route is actually graded red. The Cimes peels off in a wide cruising arc to the right, about 75 m (82 yd) from the top. The prime Vallée Blanche piste stays directly down the fall-line, veering left parallel to the chair-lift line in a wide, shallow chute, delivering this sector's highest-end blue.

All of the inter-piste terrain is open and inviting and offers the opportunity to play off wind-blown lips and kickers on the ungroomed margins, making it one of this area's prime play-grounds. Both routes eventually swing left and converge as a motorway-wide gentle schuss towards the Bergerie Kanata bar/ restaurant (see page 183) and cross-town La Cote chair lift. Keep highest left above the restaurant level and maintain momentum to head towards the on-piste cross-town link (signed as 'liaison Petite Aiguille', see page 111); or continue descending to the right of the restaurant on the steeper lower section towards the base of the Vallée Blanche chair lift (19).

The lightly wooded slopes to the right of this lower section can add a freeride flourish to the finish, otherwise the broad piste cruises down for a good link to the lift base and roadside below. Check your speed approaching this busy confluence area.

ANÉMONE

A fair red, often mogulled, flowing down the open slopes above the Bergerie Kanata bar/restaurant. Unfortunately the east-facing orientation and lack of snowmaking leave this face of the mountain prone to sparse snow cover, but it is worth a blast when conditions allow. The run can be accessed using the Bons chair lift (18), which arrives on the ridge above; or from the Vallée Blanche chair lift (19) by following the 'liaison Vallons de Bons' signs along the uppermost cross-mountain traverse. Spilling off the ridge to start, the route veers right and follows the course of a barely perceptible shallow gully, with three distinct pitches rolling over the open and undulating terrain. The line of descent bisects a cross-mountain traverse track, which is travelling from left to right to link with the Vallée Blanche piste far over to the right, otherwise the route is straightforward. Dropping out behind the Bergerie Kanata (too low to permit an on-piste link), the descent then crosses the line of the 'liaison Petite Aiguille' blue link piste, which is travelling from right to eft to the link with the core ski area. Turn left to join this (see page 111), or continue straight on down the slopes behind the Bergerie Kanata, eventually joining the lowest section of the Vallée Blanche blue to reach the base of chair lift 19.

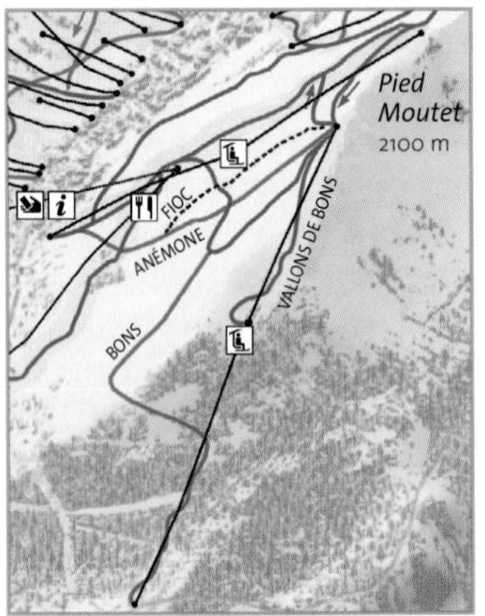

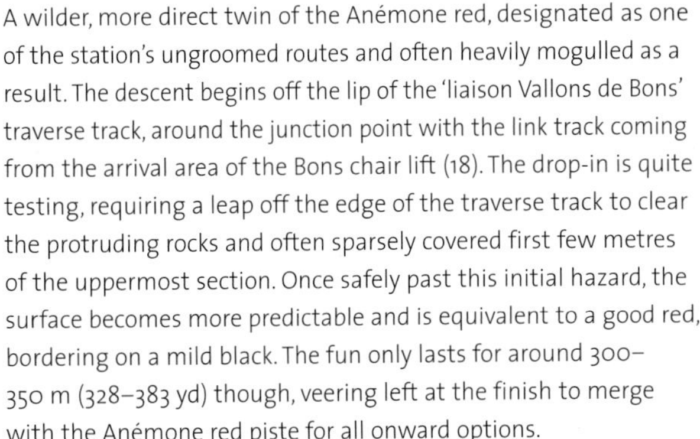

The mogulled Fioc and Anémone runs, from the Bergerie Kanata

FIOC

A wilder, more direct twin of the Anémone red, designated as one of the station's ungroomed routes and often heavily mogulled as a result. The descent begins off the lip of the 'liaison Vallons de Bons' traverse track, around the junction point with the link track coming from the arrival area of the Bons chair lift (18). The drop-in is quite testing, requiring a leap off the edge of the traverse track to clear the protruding rocks and often sparsely covered first few metres of the uppermost section. Once safely past this initial hazard, the surface becomes more predictable and is equivalent to a good red, bordering on a mild black. The fun only lasts for around 300–350 m (328–383 yd) though, veering left at the finish to merge with the Anémone red piste for all onward options.

Since this is an ungroomed route, it is at its best just after a fall of snow. At other times it is best avoided early in the morning, when the crust is frozen, and late in the afternoon, when the sun turns the snow to a dangerously heavy, porridge consistency.

VALLONS DE BONS

The uppermost cross-mountain traverse, running just below the ridge all the way from the arrival area of the Vallée Blanche chair lift (19), is signed as the 'liaison Vallons de Bons' and is in effect the upper part of this route. This flat track is the width of just one piste-basher and runs straight along the top of the mountain, with Les Deux Alpes town parallel below right. The route crosses a narrow junction at the entrance to the Fioc black, where the access track from the Bons chair lift (18) arrival point joins from above left. Carefully pass this area and continue straight out on to the ridge plateau ahead. The Anémone red piste begins to the right and there are now two alternative blue routes ahead that you can choose from:

Route A Veer left and dip over the watershed to the far side of the ridge, under the line of the two-seater Bons chair lift. This is now the Vallons de Bons piste proper. Wide and usually very quiet, this north-facing, snow-sure slope has great views (see box opposite) and is a pleasant cruise in this remote corner of the domain. This route finishes at the mid-station get-on point for the Bons chair lift, taking you up to the upper ridge again (see page 110).

Route B Continue straight on past the picnic spot at the view-point ahead (see box opposite). The entrance to the Bons red piste is just ahead on the shoulder of the hill. Stay high on the access track above the Bons entrance and follow the hairpin bend around to the right to traverse all the way across the face of the slopes. This route has sweeping views over the entire resort and traverses to the two-way La Cote chair lift, Vallée Blanche blue piste and the Bergerie Kanata bar/restaurant.

PICNIC PANORAMA

The views from this end of the Pied Moutet ridge are far-reaching. A picnic area has been set out on the ridge plateau and, on a clear day, this is a great spot to make the most of this superb viewpoint.

The deep valley below is the Gorges de l'Infernet (Gorges of Hell), housing the main access road up to Les Deux Alpes and the torrent course of the Romanche River. The two villages clinging to the mountainside opposite are Auris-en-Oisans and its namesake satellite ski station, part of the Grandes Rousses ski domain linked to Alpe d'Huez. The cable car station for the Sarenne glacier above Alpe d'Huez is visible on the summit of Pic Blanc on the horizon above right.

The town on the floor of the Romanche Valley in the distance is the regional capital le Bourg-d'Oisans. Swinging round to the right, the village of Mont-de-Lans is just below on the other side of the ridge. Below that is the Lac du Chambon, with the impressive triple-peaked summits of the Aiguilles d'Arves peeking over the skyline above.

BONS

A really worthwhile excursion, reached by running straight along the ridge plateau, past the picnic area and viewpoint above the Vallons de Bons. Swinging to the right off the shoulder of the ridge, the Bons then begins by dropping off the lip of the blue traverse route, which is leaving to the right towards the Vallée Blanche blue (clear route signs here). The village of Mont-de-Lans is directly below, with the Lac du Chambon beyond.

Peaceful birch woods on the Bons run

The Bons is immediately steep and earns its red grade easily. The upper pitch is often mogulled and gives a good workout over the lumps and bumps, with plenty of scope for variant lines on the wide slope. This side of the mountain is north-facing and holds the snow well; it is at its best mid-morning before the temperature rises. The fun extends for around 400–450 m (438–492 yd), before mellowing out and swinging left past the helipad as an easy cruise into the birch woods on a road-like track, running directly away from Les Deux Alpes. As soon as you pass under the line of the two-seater Bons chair lift (18), drop to the right to pick up a good gradient again on the sheltered, wooded slopes down the lift line. This is another nice pitch, delivering an enjoyable blast before funnelling to the right and across the road via a small pisted bridge, widening out again on the far side for the final cruise to the base of the chair lift directly below.

Overall, this is a very enjoyable run, with lots of variation and a completely different atmosphere from that of the core ski area, well away from the crowds at the most northerly margin and lowest altitude of the ski domain.

Bons red start, overlooking Mont-de-Lans and the Lac du Chambon

BONS CHAIR LIFT (18)

14¾ mins

- 760 m (2494 ft) vertical rise
- 2355 m (2576 yd) long
- 720 passengers/hour

A slow, old-fashioned and rickety chair lift serving the most northerly margin of the ski domain, accessible from the base of the Bons red run and from a mid-point get-on at the end of the principal Vallons de Bons blue. As the base-station altitude is a mere 1315 m (4313 ft), the lift platform is surfaced with dry-ski matting to ease the approach in the event of poor snow cover. The passenger-control turnstile is single file only and you need to step up on to a small, raised platform to mount the lift (assistance given). There is a piste-patrol first-aid and information point at the lift operator's cabin beside the get-on point.

The mid-point platform is reached after 9 minutes. This is a get-on point only, so remain seated with the safety bar down unless otherwise instructed by the lift operator. This mid-point get-on station is an easy link at the finish of the Vallons de Bons blue piste. The journey time from here to the top is 5¾ minutes, travelling directly above this piste.

On arrival at the top, follow the access track straight ahead, veering left to emerge cautiously at the narrow junction on the upper 'liaison Vallons de Bons' traverse. From here there are various options: either turn left to head to the Anémone and Bons reds and the Vallons de Bons blue, or turn right and carefully cross over the track to take the blue-graded 'liaison Vallée Blanche' traverse across the face of the mountain towards the principal slopes out to the far right. Alternatively, simply leap off straight ahead down the face of the mountain to begin the fairly challenging ungroomed Fioc black (see page 105).

LIAISON PETITE AIGUILLE

The sole on-piste link between the Pied Moutet sector and the core ski area on the other side of town; circuitous, but viable and well maintained, with snowmaking equipment all along the route. The link begins at the Bergerie Kanata bar/restaurant level, easily reached from any of the main pistes and traverse routes; the piste is a motorway-wide, green-equivalent cruise passing the upper end (left) of the Bergerie Kanata buildings, and is then joined/crossed by the Anémone red run from above left. The main road entering Les Deux Alpes is visible down to the right and you are now heading towards the pisted footbridge crossing it. The route swoops down to the right, with a reasonable slope angle to allow you to build momentum, descending to just above the road level and then running parallel to the road towards the bridge.

This section is very flat and often very slushy; stay alert for sudden surface changes. The pisted footbridge sometimes needs a bit of a skate to cross, but it is wide and level and should present no problem. Once across, swing right and follow the gentle pisted route for the fair link to the Petite Aiguille chair lift (2) ahead, next to La Cote chair lift which returns to the Bergerie Kanata area. You also have the option here of turning left to begin the Mont-de-Lans red run.

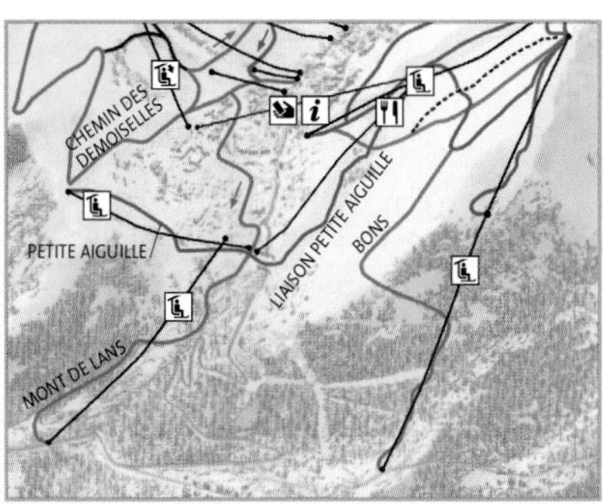

MONT-DE-LANS

Tucked away at the lowest end of Les Deux Alpes, beside the main road into town. Starting as a wide, blue-equivalent cruise, it then funnels to the right on to a simple traverse track under the line of the Mont-de-Lans chair lift (1) and into the edge of the birch woods above Monts-de-Lans village. The final section drops on to the fall-line again towards the chair-lift station. This terraced hillside has sparse snow cover, plus a couple of little ditches and clumps of vegetation to negotiate to reach the lift.

The run is worth a go at least once in good snow conditions, if just for the novelty factor of riding down to this lowest limit of the domain, although the Bons red run in the nearby Pied Moutet sector does the same and gives a longer and more consistent ride.

MONT-DE-LANS CHAIR LIFT (1)

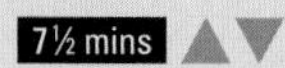

- 340 m (1116 ft) vertical rise
- 1160 m (1269 yd) long
- 560 passengers/hour

Departing from just above the main road at the upper end of Mont-de-Lans village; accessible either from the roadside or on-piste via the Monts-de-Lans red.

The journey climbs over the route of the Mont-de-Lans red run and arrives at the lower edge of Les Deux Alpes. At the top, turn left and run down the pisted access ramp. You then have the choice of either strolling over to the ski-bus stop at the roadside by the chalets to the right, or U-turning down to the left on the Petite Aiguille blue piste for a good link with the Petite Aiguille chair lift (2) just below. A 4-seater chair lift (called La Cote) will also be in place by 2006 to link with the Pied Moutet sector.

PETITE AIGUILLE CHAIR LIFT (2)

7¼ mins

- 241 m (791 ft) vertical rise
- 849 m (926 yd) long
- 1500 passengers/hour

Link lift facilitating the connection from Mont-de-Lans village and the Pied Moutet sector towards the core ski area; located at the lowest end of Les Deux Alpes, accessible via the Petite Aiguille blue and 'liaison Petite Aiguille' link route.

The control cabin is quite large and houses a ski pass kiosk. There is also a tool point, piste map and information display board beside the turnstiles. The journey up passes over the top of the upper station of the Mont-de-Lans chair lift (1) and arrives at the top of the Petite Aiguille blue piste, next to a bend on the Chemin des Demoiselles green. U-turn to the right down the lift line for the Petite Aigulle blue, or turn right and join the Chemin des Demoiselles green to traverse towards town.

ONWARD LINKS

The lower section of the Chemin des Demoiselles green route traverses towards town above the Club Med complex and residential Les 2 Alpes 1800 quarter. The track is very flat, but has just enough gradient to provide a gentle glide. Once under the line of the Village chair lift (27), you then have the choice of continuing straight on towards the central town slopes and lifts, across the beginners' zone, or you can turn down to the right to link with the Village chair lift and to reach the busy Grande Place commercial area just beyond it at Les 2 Alpes 1800.

advance.ch

CRÊTES / DIABLE SECTOR

Draped over the ridges (the *crêtes*) that run along the eastern skyline immediately above Les Deux Alpes. The majority of the station's black runs are in this sector, many of which are left ungroomed to increase the difficulty level, particularly the tricky home runs on the furrowed face of the mountain sweeping down to resort. There is also a handful of short but worthwhile reds; a couple of good blues; and a number of long green-graded traverse tracks which, as well as facilitating cross-sector links, provide adventurous beginners with an interesting excursion. The widest part of the ridge at Crêtes 2100 is a busy major interchange, housing a mid-altitude beginners' zone. A second interchange at Diable 2400 is the site of one of the station's best on-mountain restaurants (see page 184) and a spectacular paragliding launch point (see page 193).

VILLAGE CHAIR LIFT (27)

- 475 m (1559 ft) vertical rise
- 1550 m (1696 yd) long
- 2000 passengers/hour

Departing from the edge of the busy Grande Place at Les 2 Alpes 1800. Ski pass office, tool point and good information boards at the get-on level. The lift rises diagonally across the mountainside, giving sweeping views to the right across the entire resort; above the Valentin black piste and crossing over the lines of other chair lifts nearing the arrival point at the Crêtes 2100 area interchange. On arrival, dismount straight ahead on to the wide plateau.

➔ *See page 118 for orientation and onward links.*

◀ *Launching off from Diable 2400*

BELLE ÉTOILE CHAIR LIFT (26)

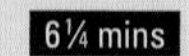

- 515 m (1690 ft) vertical rise
- 1410 m (1543 yd) long
- 1800 passengers/hour

Handy queue-jump alternative to the Jandri 1 gondola lift, based at the Alpe de Mont-de-Lans end of the town slopes and quick to reach from the Chemin des Demoiselles green and Valentin black pistes. There is a slight incline on approach to the get-on point, which has dry-ski matting to protect access in the event of slushy or sparse snow cover.

The lift travels over the Valentin black piste, under the crossing line of the Village chair lift (27) just before cresting the ridge. The entrance to the Valentin black is just below at this point, off the traversing Chemin des Demoiselles green. On arrival, there is a good view down into the Thuit Coomb beyond the fence ahead. Turn right to join the pistes flowing past the nearby piste map/information board/tool point and piste-patrol cabin to reach the Ancontres button lift (30) for the easiest link up the slope towards the Crêtes 2100 area interchange above; or keep running down the line of the arriving chair lift to the nearby Crêtes chair lift (28), linking with the Diable 2400 area interchange; or bypass this to start the Chemin des Demoiselles green and the Valentin black runs back to resort.

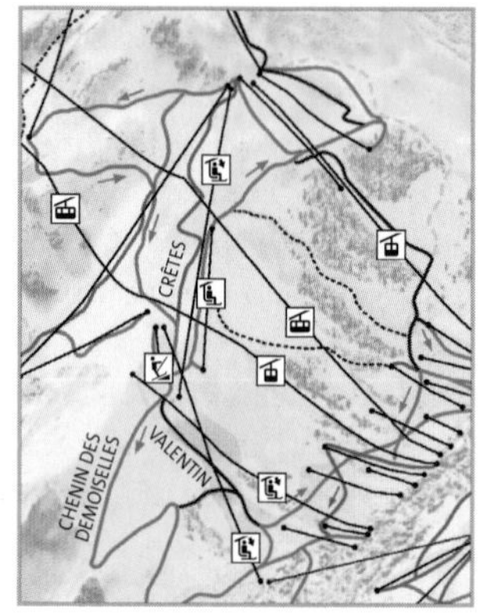

JANDRI 1 GONDOLA LIFT (25)

7½ mins

- 535 m (1755 ft) vertical rise
- 1650 m (1805 yd) long
- 1006 passengers/hour

Colloquially known as the 'white eggs', this old-fashioned 'bubble' lift is still one of the principal lifts out of the central resort area, linking with the Jandri 2 cable car via the Crêtes 2100 area interchange. It departs from a large base station just behind the central tourist office in place des 2 Alpes, at the base of the central town slopes.

Access is via a ramp up from the piste level, with plenty of frequently updated information boards beside the queue lines displaying pistes/ski-lifts accessibility, weather and avalanche risk level. The cabins are very cramped for four people; this is exacerbated by the fact that snowboards must be carried inside (only skis fit in the external gear racks) – do not be concerned if they stick out a little, but be careful not to impede the automatic doors.

Although small, the cabins have wraparound windows, letting in plenty of light and making the most of the bird's-eye views across the entire resort and town slopes. The line of travel passes almost directly above the route of the Sapins ungroomed black run, giving a good opportunity to plan your line of descent for later; nearing the arrival station, you also have a useful orientating viewpoint over the busy Crêtes 2100 area interchange.

On arrival, exit to the right; then either U-turn to the left into the forward section of the same building to board the Jandri 2 cable car (33) (see page 144), towards the Toura 2600 area interchange, or put your gear on to glide away out on the Crêtes 2100 plateau (see over for orientation). There are benches just outside the lift station to make it easier clipping in to board bindings.

CRÊTES 2100 AREA INTERCHANGE

The first of four piste and ski-lift hubs that provide a focal point for on-mountain services and links between the different sectors. Although this is a very busy crossing point, there are actually only two pistes flowing into the area: the Route de la Thuit green (see page 130), coming from the Lac du Plan area and effecting the only continuous on-piste descent from the summit of the Dôme de la Lauze; and the wide Crêtes blue piste (see page 122), coming from the neighbouring Diable 2400 area interchange.

Clear directional signage and a piste map/information post with a tool point are positioned at the heart of the plateau, clustered around La Patache bar/restaurant (see page 184), the central focus to the area. Just above and behind the restaurant are the arrival points for the two-way Village chair lift (27) and the Ancontres button lift (30). The shared Jandri 1 gondola lift (25) and Jandri 2 cable car (33) station is at the upper end of this wide and open area, overlooking the entire snowfield.

La Patache bar/restaurant at Crêtes 2100

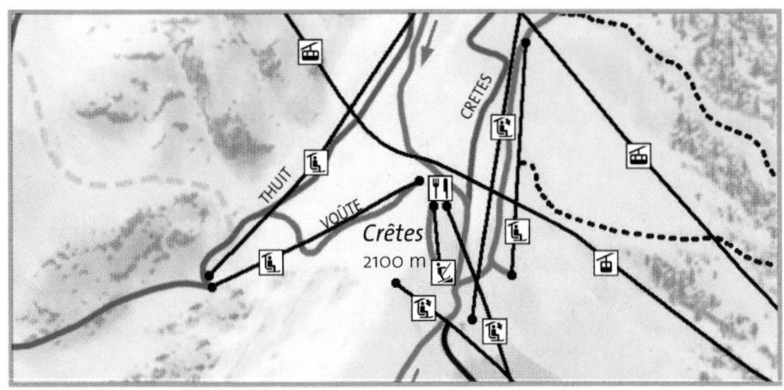

Looking towards La Patache restaurant from the Jandri lifts station, the wide beginners' zone is to the left, with piste traffic flowing past it from the Route de la Thuit behind left. To the right, at the far side of the station, is the arrival point for the Voûte chair lift (31); just to the left of that is the entrance for the Voûte red run (see page 120). For all other options, put your gear on outside the station and glide down past the restaurant.

The Crêtes blue piste is flowing in from above left, down the line of its namesake chair lift. It shares its lower slope with the shorter parallel Petites Crêtes green, served by a second parallel chair lift also called the Petites Crêtes. Both these lifts, plus the Chemin des Demoiselles green (see page 141) and the Valentin black (see page 140) home runs towards Les Deux Alpes, are reached by following the flow of the slopes down to the lower right. After 300 m (328 yd), you come to a junction point: to the right is a good link to the Crêtes chair lift (28); to the left is the get-on point for the Petites Crêtes chair lift (29). For the Chemin des Demoiselles and the Valentin pistes, keep straight on down past these lift bases, following the clear signs towards the further junction point for these two routes just ahead.

VOÛTE

A fairly worthwhile red, dropping into the wilder and quieter Thuit coomb from the contrastingly gentle and busy Crêtes 2100 area. The run starts to the left of the arrival point of the Voûte chair lift (31), a short glide from the shared Jandri 1 gondola lift (25) and Jandri 2 cable car (33) station. The entrance area and the top section of the piste are wide and gentle, picking up pace as the slope flows off the ridge, with the Voûte chair lift parallel to the right. This exposed face of the ridge often has sparse snow cover, since the wind frequently howls up the coomb and sheers off anything that is not well pisted. The fall-line to the right gives the steepest ride and usually has the best snow cover; once moguls develop this side of the piste can also take on a mild black profile. On the left-hand side there is a little gully to play in and a blue-equivalent escape track which S-bends down the slopes to take the sting out of the gradient.

The main piste really only lasts for around 250 m (274 yd), before joining the escape track that traverses across the slope from left to right to reach the lower section of the Thuit blue piste, which is flowing down the middle of the coomb. It is possible to cross the track and continue on the fall-line, over very testing and rocky ground, but make sure you do not go too low because it is a real scramble to get out of the river gully below. Stay high to the right and join the Thuit blue, turning down to the left with it for the final easy gentle schuss to link with the Thuit chair lift (32) (see page 132) and the Voûte chair lift (31), sited side by side just below. The pisted track entering this same area from ahead is the Route de la Fée blue coming from La Fée 2100. There is a piste map/information post by the lifts, with a tool point alongside.

VOÛTE CHAIR LIFT (31)

4½ mins

- 243 m (797 ft) vertical rise
- 600 m (656 yd) long
- 2400 passengers/hour

Based in the Thuit coomb, beside the Thuit chair lift (32); reached via the Voûte red, Thuit blue and Route de la Fée blue. The journey up is over the Voûte red, with views up the Thuit blue piste (see page 132) and the high cirque towards the lines of the Jandri 2 (33) and Jandri Express (55) cable cars on the skyline above left.

The chair lift arrives at the Crêtes 2100 area interchange. The entrance to the Voûte red is immediately to the right, and the shared Jandri 1 gondola lift and Jandri 2 cable-car station is to the left. La Patache bar/restaurant is straight ahead.

See page 119 for details of onward routes.

PETITE CRÊTES CHAIR LIFT (29)

6¼ mins

- 145 m (476 ft) vertical rise
- 820 m (897 yd) ong
- 900 passengers/hour

Caution – no footrests on safety bar.

Departing from the lower end of the Crêtes 2100 area and serving the Petites Crêtes green piste and giving access to the Sapins, Le Y and Diable black home runs. The views to the right on the journey up are great, sweeping over Les Deux Alpes and the Pied Moutet sector behind. On arrival, it is best to dismount to the right. U-turn right for the Petites Crêtes green (and to join the Crêtes blue); or glide over to the fence by the Jandri Express cable car pylon for the Petite Crêtes a Vallons link track towards the three black home runs on the face.

CRÊTES CHAIR LIFT (28)

6¼ mins

- 290 m (952 ft) vertical rise
- 1690 m (1849 yd) long
- 2800 passengers/hour

Busy link chair between Crêtes 2100 and Diable 2400, travelling over the Crêtes and Petites Crêtes pistes, with great views over Les Deux Alpes to the Pied Moutet sector. On arrival, go ahead right for the main Diable 2400 area interchange (see page 125), or U-turn immediately right to start the Crêtes blue and to reach the entrance to the Petit Diable red, which is by the fence below. The Crêtes blue can also be started by dismounting to the left. The Thuit chair lift (32) also arrives just above left; go under its lift lines to start the green-graded Séa Grand Nord liaison track (see page 129) towards a good red variation entrance to the Thuit blue and for the long, easy circuit through the Lac du Plan area and across the Thuit coomb back to the Crêtes 2100 area interchange.

CRÊTES

A wide and easy blue straight down the line of the Crêtes chair lift from Diable 2400. The top section is a good, fast blue, gradually mellowing in gradient and widening as it goes. Once you are level with the huge pylon for the Jandri Express cable car, near the arrival point of the Petites Crêtes chair lift (29), you can U-turn around the fence on the left to enter the Petites Crêtes a Vallons link track towards Le Y and Diable black runs. Or simply continue ahead on the Crêtes blue towards the Crêtes 2100 area interchange below. Keep highest to the right to reach La Patache restaurant and/or the Jandri 2 cable car (33).

Crêtes chair lift, on the skyline above Les Deux Alpes

DIABLE GONDOLA LIFT (23)

- 755 m (2477 ft) vertical rise
- 2235 m (2445 yd) long
- 1006 passengers/hour

An old-fashioned, bubble-style lift, colloquially known as the 'red eggs', which is the main ski lift to the core ski area from the Alpe de Venosc quarter of Les Deux Alpes. The base station is at the far end of the rue des Vikings, on the corner with rue Saint Claude (see town plan on page 65). There is a ski-bus stop outside and a pisted access track from the town slopes to within a few metres of the station's access ramp.

Pistes and lifts accessibility, weather and avalanche risk-level information is displayed inside the station. This lift gets very busy in the mornings; to ease the pressure there is a singles' line at the get-on platform to ensure that all cabins are filled to capacity,

The lift lines run horizontally for the first section leaving town, then climb up over the route of the Diable black piste, giving sweeping views over the entire town slopes area to the left and over the Vénéon Valley towards the imposing peaks of La Muzelle and the Aiguille de Venosc to the right. On arrival, exit the upper station ahead right to emerge next to the excellent Le Diable au Cœur bar/restaurant.

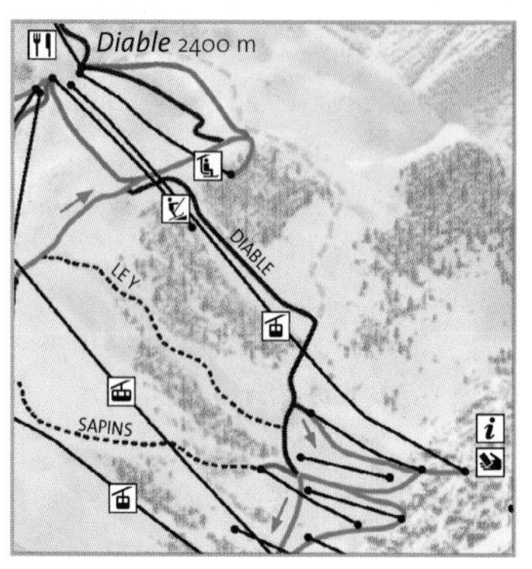

➔ *See opposite for orientation and onwards routes/links.*

DIABLE 2400 AREA INTERCHANGE

A compact ledge perched at 2400 m (7872 ft) on the flanks of the Tête Moute, with superb vistas over the Vénéon Valley. The area is focused around the upper station of the Diable gondola lift (23) and the excellent Le Diable au Cœur bar/restaurant (see page 184). As well as the Diable gondola lift, this area is also reached using the Crêtes (28), Thuit (32) and Vallons (22) chair lifts, plus the Petit Diable button lift (24), although access to the bar/restaurant level is slightly inclined from all lifts except the gondola.

The entrance to Le Diable au Cœur is almost immediately to the right when exiting the gondola station. There are deckchairs on a snow patio here, clustered around a large piste map/ information board and tool point. The Vallons chair lift arrives just in front of the terrace, which is facing south overlooking the Vénéon Valley directly towards the imposing massif of La Muzelle. From this level, you can put your gear on and immediately slide away and sweep down to the right under the terrace, out on to the wide and gentler shoulder of the mountain below.

The piste joining from above left is the well-recommended Super Diable black (see page 134). Ahead is the entrance to the Descente red piste and the Vallon de Diable off-piste route. Just to the right of these is the station's permanent paragliding operation (see page 193), which provides a spectacular launch pad into space above the deep Vénéon Valley. There is a good spot for a picnic, overlooking the launch site, out to the left. Continuing around to the right, the Super Diable chair lift (34) (see page 133) is then an easy link ahead right. Beyond this point begins the Vallons black piste down to link with the Vallons chair lift (22) (see page 128) and a cheeky back door start to the Diable black home run to Les Deux Alpes.

To get to the other side of the Diable gondola station requires a stroll or a skate against the flow of piste traffic and up an inclined slope. Once past the station building, the arrival point of the short Petit Diable button lift (24) is immediately to the left, next to the entrance to the Petit Diable red piste which accesses the Diable black piste (see page 139).

The Crêtes blue piste (see page 122) dips away ahead left towards the Crêtes 2100 area interchange, down the line of the Crêtes chair lift (28) arriving on slightly higher ground ahead. Highest to the right is the arrival point of the Thuit chair lift (32). The green-graded Séa Grand Nord link route (see page 129) begins beneath the lines of the Thuit chair lift, a short walk uphill from the Diable station level; this route accesses a lovely red-graded higher-altitude variation start to the excellent Thuit blue run; less experienced visitors can ues this route to make a long but easily manageable circuit via the Lac du Plan area, across the impressive Thuit coomb and all the way to the Crêtes 2100 area interchange.

Le Diable au Cœur bar/restaurant at the Diable 2400 area interchange

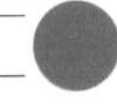

DESCENTE

A short and fairly tame red which is noteworthy because it provides access to the lower Vallons du Diable off-piste route and also because it dips towards the Vénéon Valley, giving spectacular views across to the impressive peaks of La Muzelle and the Aiguille de Venosc. The run begins to the left of the paragliding launch pads at Diable 2400, straight off the shoulder of the mountain. It then swings around to the right, beneath the paragliders take-off point, maintaining a fair slope angle around to the face of the mountain towards the Vallons chair lift (22), merging with the end of the Petites Crêtes a Diable green-graded link track for the final approach to the lift.

Paragliding over the Vénéon Valley

The Vallons du Diable off-piste route mirrors the upper part of the Descente piste, but dips lower to the left, taking a more vertigo-inducing route closer to the edge of the precipice into the valley. This route bypasses the Vallons chair lift (22) and continues below the tree line, eventually swinging right to join the lower section of the Diable black piste for the home run to Les Deux Alpes. The full classic Vallons du Diable descent actually begins much higher off the left-hand side of the Super Diable black piste. To discover this and many more exiting itineraries, contact the Bureau des Guides (see page 76 for contact details).

VALLONS

A very short black, really a standard red, which provides a little-known back-door entrance to the better Diable black piste. Access is straightforward: swoop down under the terrace of the Diable au Cœur bar/restaurant, past the get-on point for the Super Diable chair lift (34), and head towards the line of the Vallons chair lift (22). Ahead right, under the lift line, is an unmarked link over to join the nearby Petit Diable red for access to the Diable black; otherwise, turn left under the lift line for the Vallons piste. After a short, easy access track, the Vallons picks up pace by dropping on to the fall-line on the wide, open slope. Unfortunately this lasts for no more than 200 m (219 yd) before it peters out to join the link track for the final approach to the chair lift. It is also possible to traverse past the lift to join the Diable black out to the right.

VALLONS CHAIR LIFT (22)

4¼ mins

- 251m (824 ft) vertical rise
- 675 m (739 yd) long
- 1030 passengers/hour

An old lift providing a link up to the Diable 2400 area interchange from the bottom of the Descente red and Vallons black pistes and from the end of the Petites Crêtes a Vallons link track. Stay alert for the kick that the chairs have at the get-on point. On arrival, dismount straight ahead and then U-turn down to the right to link with the Super Diable chair lift (34), start the Descente red or Vallons black, or to reach the paragliding operation. Alternatively, turn immediately left for the Diable au Cœur bar/restaurant and the Diable 2400 area interchange.

➔ *See page 126 for orientation and onward links*

SÉA GRAND NORD

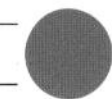

Although just a link from the Diable 2400 area interchange to the Lac du Plan area, this road-like traverse is noteworthy because it gives access to a higher, red-graded start to one of the best blue runs in the domain, the Thuit. Also, when linked with the Route de la Thuit green, it provides beginners with an interesting first adventure through some wilder scenery.

The route begins just under the arrival point for the Thuit chair lift (32), at the Diable 2400 area interchange, easily reached on arrival from that lift or the Crêtes chair lift (28), but a short inclined stroll or skate from the Diable gondola lift station. The directional signs are subtitled as 'liaison Diable a Lac du Plan' and the route is well maintained and easy to follow. About 250 m (274 yd) from the start, the red-graded upper variation of the excellent Thuit blue drops away into the coomb to the left (see page 131); otherwise keep straight on.

The rest of the route runs gently through the wild and rocky scenery of this glacially carved landscape, eventually swinging to the left and dipping down with a slightly steeper pitch to the edge of the Lac du Plan tarn, by the base of the Bellecombes chair lift (see page 137), joined by traffic from the right exiting from the Grand Couloir black run. To continue the circuit to the Crêtes 2100 area interchange, follow the signs for the Route de la Thuit green route through the cutting ahead left (see over).

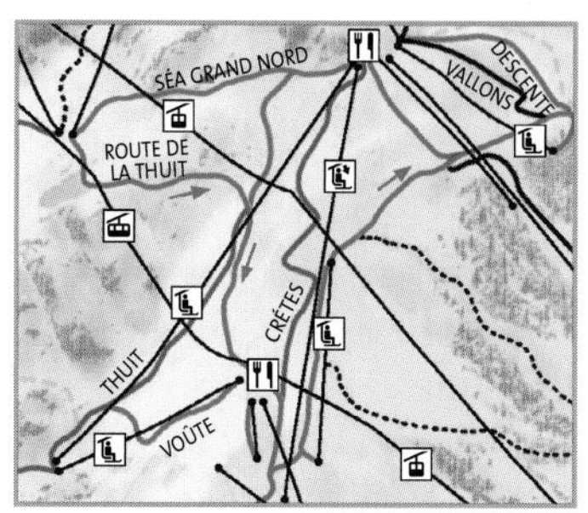

ROUTE DE LA THUIT

Starting from the Lac du Plan area, behind the get-on point for the Bellecombes chair lift (see page 137), this gentle and circuitous track has the distinction of being the sole link route through this section of the ski domain, facilitating the only continuous on-piste summit-to-base descent.

It is reached via the Séa Grand Nord green link route, the Grand Couloir black, and from any of the routes joining the Grand Nord blue into the Lac du Plan area. It funnels out of the Lac du Plan tarn depression through a cutting in the crest of the ridge to emerge high on the flanks of the Thuit coomb. This point is a severely busy bottleneck in the pistes network and the piste surface gets very choppy very quickly each day because of heavy traffic. It really should be considered as a blue route, but should present no nasty surprises for confident and progressing beginners.

As soon as it has emerged into the coomb, the route swings wide to the left and follows the contour-line in an arc around the upper sweep of the cirque. Almost immediately to the right there is a really inviting steep drop-off for advanced riders to shortcut down to the Thuit blue below (see opposite). At the mid point of the sweep across the cirque the route crosses the wide entrance to the Thuit blue (see page 132), which is one of the best blues in the domain. The steep piste joining from above left at this point is a red-graded higher start for the Thuit, accessed via the Séa Grand Nord (see previous page).

The rest of the Route de la Thuit green is very straightforward, simply continuing on the contour line ahead and flowing out into the upper end of the wide snowfield at the Crêtes 2100 area interchange (see page 118 for orientation and onward links); keep highest to the right to reach the Jandri 2 cable car station.

DÉVERSOIR SHORTCUT

A great initiation to off-piste for more advanced ability visitors. The descent is a good black equivalent, with a slightly tamer option of a marked black route taking the most popular line. It begins off the right-hand lip of the upper section of the Route de la Thuit green, on the upper arc of the cirque in the Thuit coomb. You can pick almost any point to drop off on to the immediately steep and rocky slope, or follow the marked route of the parallel Déversoir black. Check first that there is enough snow cover and plan your line well. The descent finishes across a little stream gully at the edge of the Thuit blue piste, allowing you to swoop down to the right and enjoy the lower section of this fine blue piste towards the Thuit (32) and Voûte (31) chair lifts.

THUIT (VARIATION)

The Thuit blue piste (see page 132) is one of the best blue runs in the domain and this red-graded variant extends the fun by giving a higher altitude start. Take the Séa Grand Nord green (see page 129) from the Diable 2400 area interchange. Shortly after the start the entrance to this red route peels off to the left. The top section flows off the shoulder of the ridge to develop a really enjoyable fall-line descent down into the Thuit coomb. The piste officially finishes where it meets the Route de la Thuit green, which is traversing from right to left, but the major attraction is simply to keep going on the wider Thuit blue piste, which continues ahead as an uninterrupted descent.

! Take care crossing the busy traffic on the Route de la Thuit.

THUIT

One of the best high-end blue runs in Les Deux Alpes ski domain, slicing directly down the middle of the Thuit coomb, a massive glacially formed chute contained by an impressive cirque of craggy ridges. The piste officially begins at a wide entrance in the middle of the coomb, pouring off the mid-point curve of the Route de la Thuit (see previous page), but can be extended by beginning off the higher Séa Grand Nord green route (see page 130). Advanced visitors can also drop in using the Déversoir shortcut (see previous page). The main Thuit piste is motorway wide and delivers a mild red profile to start if conditions are chopped up, developing into a fast cruise straight down the line of the Thuit chair lift (32) to schuss out for a good link with that lift and the neighbouring Voûte chair lift (see page 121). Keep to the left-hand side at the bottom to maintain momentum for the flat run-out to the lifts.

THUIT CHAIR LIFT (32)

11 mins

- 450 m (1477 ft) vertical rise
- 1500 m (1641 yd) long
- 1450 passengers/hour

Departing from the bottom of the Thuit coomb, next to the Voûte chair lift, and reached by the Thuit and Route de la Fée blues and the Voûte red; piste map/information post and tool point at the get-on area. The lift travels directly up the route of the Thuit blue, up the middle of the cirque and over a small col, to emerge at the Diable 2400 area interchange. On arrival, turn right for all main options from the interchange area (see page 125 for orientation and onward links). U-turn down to the right and go under the arriving lift-lines to reach the Séa Grand Nord (see page 129).

SUPER DIABLE CHAIR LIFT (34)

- 390 m (1280 ft) vertical rise
- 1110 m (1214 yd) long
- 2200 passengers/hour

A noteworthy lift for advanced-ability riders, who will appreciate the access it provides to the most reliable black runs in the domain (including the classic Vallon du Diable off-piste route), as well as for competent novices who can share in the buzz of this wilder terrain yet bypass the black runs to reach the Toura 2600 area interchange via a blue link route.

The lift departs from the Diable 2400 area interchange and is based just below the level of the Diable au Cœur bar/restaurant terrace, a short and good link from the main interchange level. The trip up goes straight up the line of the Super Diable black piste, giving you a perfect opportunity to check out the lie of the land and plan your descent.

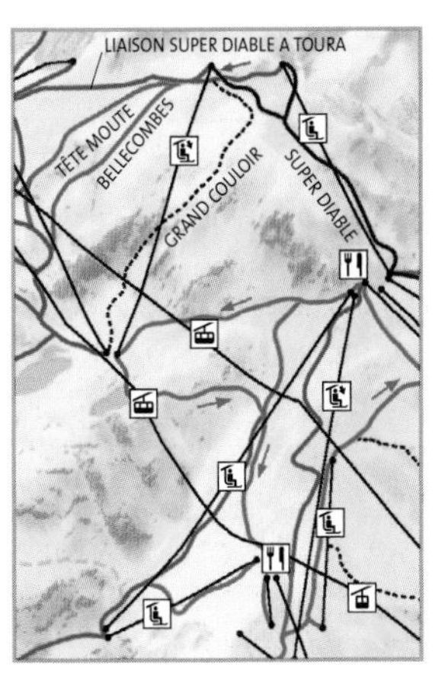

On arrival, dismount ahead via the steepish off-ramp and turn right on to the reasonably wide and flat pitch just below the summit of Tête Moute, the most important peak in this sector of the ski domain. The Super Diable starts directly down the fall-line. The blue link route towards the Toura 2600 area interchange is down this shared start a little and then to the right, swinging under the line of the arriving lift.

SUPER DIABLE

Before being tamed as a pisted route, this was one of the most mythical off-piste descents in Europe; it continues to draw enthusiasts, especially for the access it provides to the still-extreme classic Vallon du Diable off-piste descent, which dances along the edge of the precipice above the Vénéon Valley. To discover that and many more exiting itineraries, contact the Bureau des Guides (see page 76).

The Super Diable has a straightforward route – straight down! It is a fast, motorway-wide blast, equivalent to a high-end red. It is usually well pisted and the sub-glacial altitude ensures that snow conditions are reliable. At the finish, keep left to stay out of the traffic at the Diable 2400 area interchange. Veering left to link with the Descente red (see page 127) to the Vallons chair lift (22) is the most enjoyable way to reach the main interchange level and onward links.

LIAISON SUPER DIABLE A TOURA

A gentle link route from the top of the Super Diable chair lift (34) (see page 133) around to the Toura 2600 area interchange, passing the entrances to some more serious routes on the way. Begin by gliding wide to the right at the shared start area beside the Super Diable black piste, leaving that to swing to the right under the arriving lift-lines and remain on the contour-line. The route is then a gentle trundle, passing the entrance to the Grand Couloir black (see opposite) and then the Bellecombes and Tête Moute reds (see page 136). As soon as you approach the interchange at Toura 2600, turn hard right to link to the Snow Park; or continue straight ahead to ride out into the middle of the interchange area

➔ *See page 146 for orientation and onward links.*

GRAND COULOIR

An ungroomed ride down a wide and rocky couloir above the Lac du Plan area, with a hint of off-piste to its character. It is accessed from the Liaison Super Diable a Toura traverse from the Super Diable chair lift (34) (see opposite) or the Bellecombes chair lift (see page 137). The approach is over an open expanse of undulating terrain spread out below the Liaison Super Diable a Toura track. Go furthest to the left to reach the drop-in point. You are free to pick any line and there is plenty of scope for playing off the sides – the left-hand wall gives the best challenge. The steep and testing mid-section is the crux of the descent, but lasts for no more than 300–350 m (328–383 yd). Do not go too low or you will have to hike out. Instead, once you are directly under the lines of the high overhead Jandri Express cable car and the closer Bellecombes chair lift, swing left and stay high to traverse along the contour-line, parallel to the line of the chair lift. Check your speed as you approach the chair-lift base to merge with the Séa Grand Nord green route for the final few metres to the lift. As well as linking with the Bellecombes chair lift, you additionally have the option to continue straight on to start the Route de la Thuit green (see page 130).

Liaison Super Diable a Toura track towards the entrance for the Grand Couloir (ahead left)

BELLECOMBES / TÊTE MOUTE

Twin red motorways on the open and undulating flanks of the Tête du Diable, delivering short but fast on-piste cruises and a myriad of good inter-piste possibilities, making this a great style-honing area for early intermediates. Used in conjunction with the new fast six-seater declutchable Bellecombes chair lift, this often overlooked area allows for almost non-stop circuits, away from the crowds that gravitate to the glitzier, and still conveniently close, Toura 2600 zone. Both pistes are also reachable via the Liaison Super Diable a Toura link track (see page 134).

Both pistes descend to the right of the chair lift line, the Tête Moute furthest right; a bank of higher ground separates the two runs and provides lovely freeriding terrain on powder days. Both routes have wide and easily accessible entrances, but the Bellecombes piste offers the better slope angle at the top section, the right-hand side having the steepest profile. Shortly after the uppermost pitch, both routes veer towards one another, usually with a couple of pisted crossover connections. The Tête Moute is also joined from the right by the Grand Nord Bis and Grand Nord blues. All pistes blend together below in a huge convergence area and funnel through a chicane of speed-control fencing before flowing on to a very gentle straight, heading directly across the flat Lac du Plan tarn depression to link with the Bellecombes chair lift ahead left.

Other options from this area include swinging to the right just as you approach the Lac du Plan, to start the Route de la Fée blue link to La Fée (see page 155); or continuing straight past the Bellecombes chair lift get-on point, to pick up the Route de la Thuit green (see page 130) into the Thuit coomb and facilitating the continuous descent to Les Deux Alpes resort.

BELLECOMBES CHAIR LIFT

4¼ mins

- 430 m (1411 ft) vertical rise
- 1285 m (1406 yd) long
- 3300 passengers/hour

A recent and welcome improvement to the ski-lift network, departing from the Lac du Plan area and serving the Grand Couloir black (see page 135) and the Bellecombes and Tête Moute reds, as well as providing an albeit flat link to the Toura 2600 area interchange via the Liaison Super Diable a Toura track.

The lift is reached by the Séa Grand Nord green traverse (see page 129) and by all variations of the Grand Nord blues (see page 154), as well as by all of the above-mentioned pistes.

The journey begins horizontally across the tarn. This is used as a feeder reservoir for the snowmaking equipment; the bubbles breaking the surface are created by a loop of underwater hoses which agitate the water to help prevent it from developing a thick ice cover, thus keeping the water supply accessible. Once it reaches the far shore, the lift climbs up the rocky chute containing the ungroomed Grand Couloir black, providing a moving vantage point to check out the best lines of descent.

On arrival, U-turn either right or left down the lift line to the Liaison Super Diable a Toura track just below. Turn right and follow that for the flat traverse to the Toura 2600 area interchange, or simply veer right and cross the track to reach the nearby Bellecombes and Tête Moute reds. To reach the Grand Couloir black, U-turn to the right off the lift and then range across the open snowfields towards the highest ground ahead left (see picture on page 135). Traverse furthest left for a 'back-door' link to the Super Diable black (see page 134), although this is a very laborious way of reaching that piste.

HOME RUNS

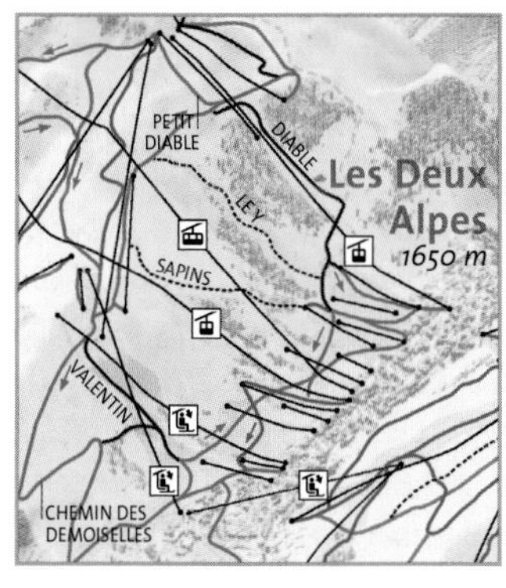

Les Deux Alpes has accessible slopes directly above the resort that flow into the town slopes to provide home runs. These are some of the toughest on-piste descents in the domain, particularly in the afternoon when the sun has turned the snow to the consistency of porridge. The most viable routes on the mountain are all black, although the Valentin piste can be regarded as a good red. There is also a green home run – the Chemin des Demoiselles (see page 141); although this is long and flat and prone to poor snow cover, on the right day in the right conditions it opens up the mountain for all visitors to enjoy the thrill of riding from summit to base.

PETIT DIABLE

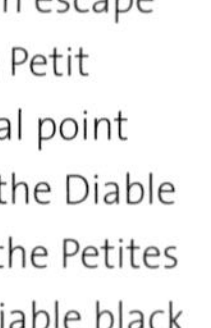

A short, decent red link towards the Diable black, with an escape route to the Vallons chair lift (22) (see page 128) and the Petit Diable button lift (24). The route begins beside the arrival point of button lift 24, off the entrance for the Crêtes blue at the Diable 2400 area interchange. It drops straight down to meet the Petites Crêtes a Vallons green link, where the entrance to the Diable black is slightly inclined to the right. With good snow cover you can drop off ahead to join the upper section. Alternatively, simply turn left and flow with the gentle link track towards the lifts.

DIABLE

Regarded as one of the signature routes at Les Deux Alpes but, unfortunately, prone to poor snow cover on its south-westerly orientated slopes. The route can be started using the Petit Diable red piste from the Diable 2400 area interchange but officially begins off the flat Petites Crêtes a Vallons green link, which traverses across from a point beside the pylon for the Jandri Express cable car, at the arrival level of the Petites Crêtes chair lift (29) (see page 121). The best way in, though, is to approach on the Vallons black piste (see page 128) from the Diable 2400 area interchange, a route that provides the most consistent slope angle.

The Diable piste hugs the pylon line of its namesake gondola lift, taking a direct but often patchy fall line until it reaches a clearly defined cut to the right, heading towards town. The Vallon du Diable off-piste route joins from where the Diable piste turns right. The final approach to resort is well signed and allows you to traverse to virtually any point along the town slopes strip.

LE Y (pronounced 'Luh-e-grec')

Along with the Sapins, this is one of the most challenging of the home runs. Like the Diable, it is accessed using the Petites Crêtes a Vallons green link track from beside the huge pylon for the Jandri Express, traversing out to the left across the top of the hill before dropping straight down and funnelling through a narrower, ungroomed, mogulled swath through the tree line, and then widening out for the final thigh-burning workout veering towards the Alpe de Venosc end of the town slopes below. Stay high enough and you can glide to virtually any point at the base of the pistes along the edge of the resort.

SAPINS

Accessed mid-way down the Crêtes blue (see page 122), off the parallel Petites Crêtes green, reachable on-piste from Diable 2400 or using the Petites Crêtes chair lift (29) (see page 121) from Crêtes 2100; the entrance is under the line of the Jandri 1 gondola lift (the 'white eggs').

Similar in profile to Le Y, this tough, ungroomed descent is often mogulled and is wide enough to allow a host of different rides, from the almost pisted surface on the most popular lines to the deeper powder pockets at either side, the huge gully to the right beckoning advanced riders. Once at the top of the town slopes, you can traverse to almost any point along the base area.

VALENTIN

An excellent, well-maintained piste that is by far the most reliable and versatile home run. When snow conditions soften in the early afternoons it can be regarded as a reasonably challenging red.

Accessed from the lower end of the Crêtes 2100 area interchange (see page 118), through a busy bottleneck between the Crêtes (28) and Petites Crêtes (29) chair lifts, the approach is via the shared start for the Chemin des Demoiselles green. The Valentin entrance is easy to spot beside the snowmaking equipment platform, after the final lift lines. The piste drops straight down the face, parallel to the Belle Étoile chair lift pylons. The big gully to the left is a testing adventure for more advanced riders. Stick to the main piste for an enjoyable workout – the left-hand side gives the steepest line. At the bottom, either veer right to reach the Grand Place at Les 2 Alpes 1800, or veer left on to the traverse track towards the town slopes. The run can be ridden in circuits using the Belle Étoile chair lift (26) (see page 116).

CHEMIN DES DEMOISELLES

A lengthy and circuitous trek with long, flat traverses and switchback bends, descending wide above and beyond Les 2 Alpes 1800. The Chemin is a dirt track in summer, cut in to the mountainside to provide off-road vehicle and mountain bike access. In the winter, as well as serving as a green-graded home run, this is also the route taken for evening snowmobile excursions (see page 192).

Although the route is viable, it is prone to poor snow cover. The patchy surface and narrow width make it hard work, but in good conditions it does allows confident beginners to make the on-piste home run to resort.

Access is from the lower end of the Crêtes 2100 area interchange (see page 118), following the waymarked track towards the junction point for the Valentin black piste. Unfortunately, this section is a real bottleneck, particularly towards the end of day when most people are heading back to the resort. After you pass under the final chair lift lines, the Valentin piste drops off to the left and the Chemin des Demoiselles continues traversing straight on out to the far right. The route is well defined and easy to follow, taking a couple of hairpin bends to wind its way languidly towards town. There are a couple of options at the lower bends. The first is to link with the lower section of the Valentin black; the second, at the arrival level of the Petite Aiguille chair lift (2), is to take the Petite Aiguille blue piste towards the start of the Mont-de-Lans red run to Mont-de-Lans village, or to link with La Cote chair lift to the Pied Moutet sector. Otherwise, simply remain on the Chemin to reach the Grand Place area at Les 2 Alpes 1800 ahead, or to continue straight on towards the main town slopes.

TOURA / LA FÉE SECTORS

These are two contrasting sectors at the centre of Les Deux Alpes' ski domain, offering two very different atmospheres and skiing experiences. Toura 2600, the geographical and social heart of the ski area, is focused around the station's excellent Snow Park (see page 151). La Fée 2100, out at the margins of the ski area, is more peaceful and less developed. The two sectors are intertwined and provide a welcome contrast to the much narrower, linear form of the rest of the upper ski area.

JANDRI EXPRESS 1 CABLE CAR (55)

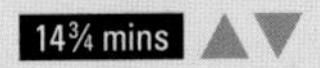

- 930 m (3051 ft) vertical rise
- 4100 m (4485 yd) long
- 1800 passengers/hour

When is a cable car not a cable car? When it is a giant gondola! The lift mechanism declutches the cabins from the haul cable and they move slowly through the stations. This is the arterial lift for Les Deux Alpes' core ski area; the huge base station is located at the top right of the place des 2 Alpes in the centre of town. The first-floor entrance is reached via an access ramp from the ground level. The ski pass control cabin and turnstiles are at the lower end of the ramp to ease congestion, but this is still a very busy bottle-neck in the mornings.

The journey up gives commanding views over the resort and town slopes and then the entire Crêtes 2100 area interchange, before passing high above the Thuit coomb and arriving at the Toura 2600 area interchange

➔ *See page 144 for orientation and onward links.*

◀ ***Chalet de la Toura terrace towards the Snow Park***

JANDRI 2 CABLE CAR (33)

5¾ mins

- 405 m (1329 ft) vertical rise
- 2420 m (2653 yd) long
- 850 passengers/hour

Connects the Crêtes 2100 area interchange and the Toura 2600 area interchange. The base-station building is shared with the arriving Jandri 1 gondola lift (25), but you need to exit one station before you can enter the other. Current lift and piste information is displayed at the base entrance area. Once through the control gates you can board the first available cabin from either side of the cramped platforms. If you have descended using this lift, turn immediately left on arrival and exit via the steps directly off the platform; the Jandri 1 is then the second entrance on the right and the rest of the Crêtes 2100 area interchange is spread out ahead below (see page 118 for orientation and onward links).

The cabins travel at a vertigo-inducing height over the Thuit coomb and Lac du Plan area. In the summer season, the lift stops at the highest mid-point and you can bungy jump 140 m (459 ft) into the void below! On arrival at the upper station, there are directional signs on the wall of the piste-patrol cabin ahead outside. The Jandri Express cable car station is also straight ahead beyond that (see page 146 for orientation and onward links).

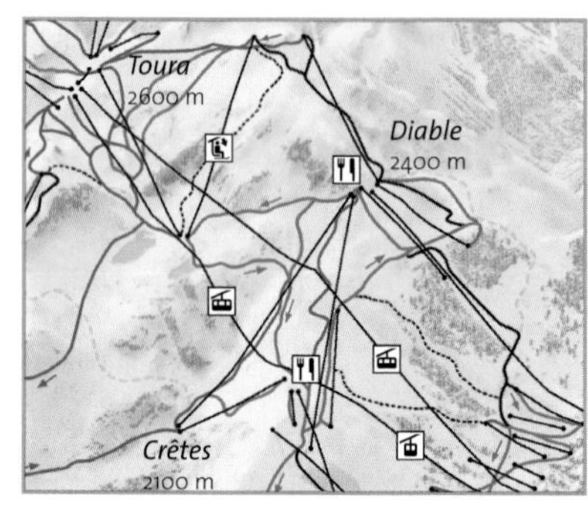

TOURA 2600 AREA INTERCHANGE

With two excellent restaurants and its proximity to the world-class and innovative Snow Park and Slide zones, this area is not only the geographical centre of the ski domain but also the pulsing heart of the station for most of the day. The altitude (2600 m/ 8528 ft) also ensures that the surrounding slopes are snow-sure yet less exposed than the glacial zone, which is another reason why this area is so popular. The interchange is sited at a narrow bottleneck in the pistes network and virtually all on-piste traffic descending from the summit glacier and the Slide zones needs to pass through this area. This is also the sole interchange for the lifts from the lower sectors to link with those connecting with the uppermost Glacier 3200 area interchange.

The Toura 2600 area is arranged on two distinct levels. The main lift stations are on higher ground along with Le Panoramic bar/restaurant. Below these, the wide, flat floor of a huge snow-bowl houses the big Chalet de la Toura bar/restaurant, a picnic area, the chair lifts serving the Snow Park and Boarder/SkierCross courses, and receives the incoming pistes from the glacier and the Slide zones. The lower level is connected with the upper level by a short rope tow (lift 41), with an equally short, easy piste running parallel in the opposite direction alongside.

Toura 2600 area interchange

UPPER TOURA 2600 LEVEL

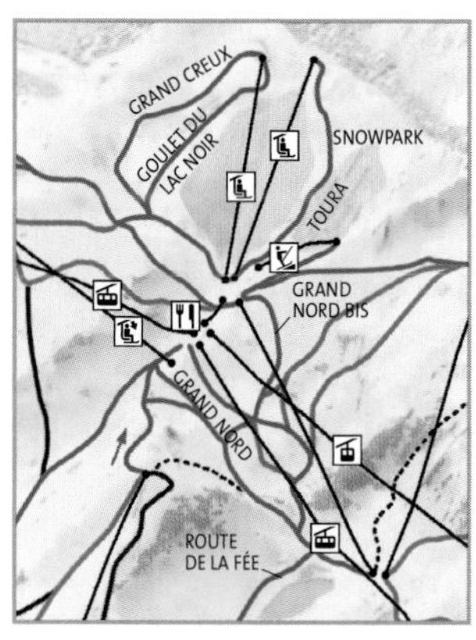

The Jandri Express cable cars are the principal lifts in the ski domain and their massive, shared mid-station dominates the skyline at Toura 2600. Arriving at this altitude from the Jandri Express 1 (55) brings you to the upper level at the interchange, where a cluster of linking ski lifts and Le Panoramic bar/restaurant are located. On exiting from the Jandri Express 1, immediately to your left in the forward half of the same station is the Jandri Express 2 (56) (see page 161) towards the Glacier 3200 area interchange. It is possible to put your gear on here and glide away down the short link piste straight ahead, parallel to the line of the Retour rope tow (41), to reach the huge lower plateau level below (see page 148).

The piste travelling towards the Jandri Express station from ahead right is the Liaison Super Diable a Toura blue link, merged with traffic returning from the top of l'Envers button lift (40) at the Snow Park. This link piste glides around the side of the Jandri Express 1 station building and under the arriving lift lines. Steps there access the Jandri Express 1 return platform towards Les Deux Alpes.

At the far side of the station is a flat, open area housing a centrally positioned piste patrol cabin, with a tool point and plenty of directional signs fixed to its walls. Beyond that is the

upper station for the Jandri 2 cable car (33) (see page 144). Passengers arriving on this lift have to stroll around to the far side of the Jandri Express station ahead to reach the entrance for the Jandri Express 2 (see page 161), as well as for the link piste down to the lower level of the interchange to head towards the Snow Park; passengers can also shortcut under the uppermost lift lines to reach the rear of the Chalet de la Toura bar/restaurant below.

The third building on the upper level at Toura 2600 is Le Panoramic bar/restaurant (see page 186), located beyond the Jandri 2 cable car station, furthest away from the Jandri Express station. The eight-seater Glaciers chair lift (42) (see page 162), connecting with the Glacier 3200 area interchange, is reached via a short, blue-graded link piste behind Le Panoramic.

From the area around Le Panoramic and between the two cable car stations, you can ride on-piste in two directions: flow off to the west (towards Les Deux Alpes) to the Grand Nord blue (see page 154), down the face of the mountain towards the Lac du Plan area, or glide off the high ground in the opposite direction to join the piste emerging from the tunnel below right (coming from the lower, wider plateau level); flowing away from the tunnel takes you to a junction point just ahead. Continuing straight on is the Gours blue towards La Fée (see page 156); peeling off to the left is a variation of the Grand Nord blue.

Le Panoramic Toura

LOWER TOURA 2600 LEVEL

The main focus for pistes convergence and services provision at this interchange, contained within a huge snowbowl, the pisted floor of which is a wide, sunken plateau, designated as a picnic area. The area is overlooked by the excellent Snow Park, served by the Toura (38) and Lac Noir (39) chair lifts, which rise from the floor of the snowbowl, furthest away from the cable cars and requiring a stroll to reach unless you are descending into this area on-piste. The pistes entering from above left of these lifts are the Brêche red, the Jandri blue and the merged Grand Creux blue and Goulet du Lac Noir blue. The Brêche and Jandri pistes also have a joint spur bypassing the flat snowbowl floor, traversing higher on the sidewall for a fair link with the Upper Toura 2600 level.

The only other viable on-piste route to Toura 2600 is via the Liaison Super Diable a Toura blue, which runs to the Upper Toura 2600 level and also allows a shortcut to the Snow Park lifts via the steep sidewall of the snowbowl.

At the other side of this wide and sheltered depression, nearest to the cable car stations, is the popular Chalet de la Toura bar/restaurant (see page 186). This massive log cabin is the social hub of the interchange and is usually buzzing from late morning to late afternoon. Public WCs are located at the rear of the building, accessible externally at lower ground floor level.

For all onward links out of the Toura 2600 area, either take the Retour rope tow (41) at the side of the Chalet de la Toura terrace, to reach the upper lifts level, or go through the tunnel past the other side of the restaurant to access the Gours blue (see page 156) and the Grand Nord blue (see page 154).

Welcome to the Slide universe, Les Deux Alpes' Snow Park

Slide

TOURA CHAIR LIFT (38)

7¼ mins

- 240 m (787 ft) vertical rise
- 1050 m (1149 yd) long
- 2400 passengers/hour

The right-hand one of the two chair lifts serving the Snow Park (see opposite), best for accessing the Big Air jumps, the Halfpipe and the rails' zone. There is a magic carpet at the get-on point. The trip up gives a bird's-eye view of the main park to the right and the main Boarder/SkierCross and Freecross courses to the left. On arrival, the dismount area at the top of the Toura ridge is flat and wide, with great views into the Vénéon Valley beyond. U-turn to the right for the Toura blue piste (see page 152), descending parallel to the left of this lift line. You can then traverse to the right to reach the Boarder/SkierCross and Freecross courses, or ride left for a good run-in to the main Snow Park.

LAC NOIR CHAIR LIFT (39)

7½ mins

- 265 m (870 ft) vertical rise
- 1030 m (1127 yd) long
- 1500 passengers/hour

The left-hand one of the two chair lifts serving the Snow Park, best for accessing the main Boarder/SkierCross and Freecross courses. The lift travels directly above the Freecross course and also gives good orientating views over the main Snow Park to the right. On arrival, dismount straight ahead to clear the counterweight pylon. There are good directional signs ahead and a panoramic picnic spot beyond. Turn left for the flat traverse to the start of the Grand Creux blue, or U-turn right to begin the Goulet du Lac Noir blue (see page 152). Keep right for the Boarder/SkierCross and Freecross courses, or ride wide left for the Toura blue and the main Snow Park.

SNOW PARK

Les Deux Alpes' Snow Park is one of Europe's largest and most progressive. The station takes 'new-school' snowsports very seriously, as evidenced by its commitment to the freestyle ethos and its innovative Slide zones, accessed from the higher Glacier 3200 area interchange and flowing down to the main Snow Park area. The buzz and ambiance of the Snow Park and Slide zones are also mirrored in the resort by the affiliated Slide Planet Café near the central place des 2 Alpes (see page 201).

The Snow Park is located on the open slopes of a huge snowbowl just above the Toura 2600 area interchange and is served by two chair lifts (see opposite). These are currently only non-declutchable lifts but they are reasonably efficient, the only drawback being that they are a flat walk from/to the nearest bar/restaurant and link lifts. The rails/boxes' zone of the park is served by the further l'Envers button lift (40). This can also be used to gain height to bypass the flat floor of the snowbowl for an on-piste link to the cable car stations.

All of the park's modules offer a good in-line run and flow back to the base of the two dedicated chair lifts (see over for features).

Les Deux Alpes Snow Park at Toura 2600

SNOW PARK MODULES AND FEATURES

- 2 Boarder/SkierCross courses (1 especially for children/novices)
- 1 Freecross course (natural banked turns)
- 1 Full-size halfpipe
- 1 Axe Pipe with 6 sub-modules
- 3 Slope styles
- 10+ Rails and boxes
- 1 Quarterpipe
- 2–3 Big Air launch pads
- 10+ Tables and hips
- Chill zone and music hut

TOURA

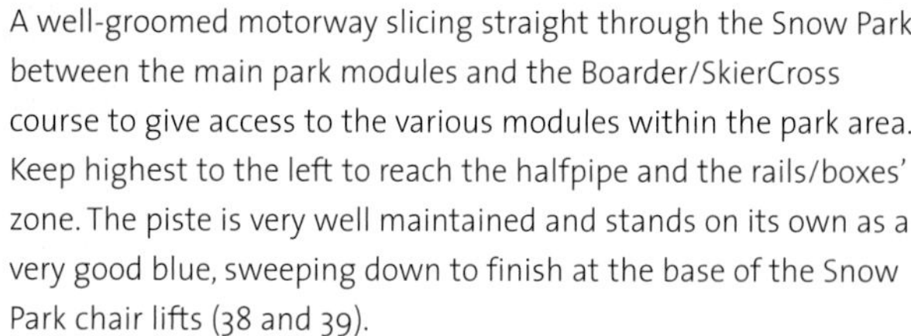

A well-groomed motorway slicing straight through the Snow Park between the main park modules and the Boarder/SkierCross course to give access to the various modules within the park area. Keep highest to the left to reach the halfpipe and the rails/boxes' zone. The piste is very well maintained and stands on its own as a very good blue, sweeping down to finish at the base of the Snow Park chair lifts (38 and 39).

GRAND CREUX/GOULET DU LAC NOIR

Running wide to the right of the Freecross and main Border/Skier-Cross courses, the Grand Creux is a straightforward standard blue in a wide arc to the high right. The steeper Goulet du Lac Noir piste runs closest the Freecross course and is often mogulled, bordering on a fair red. Both routes merge to finish along with the Jandri blue flowing towards the Snow Park lifts and across the floor of the snowbowl towards the Toura 2600 area interchange.

Clear, funky signs are a feature of Les Deux Alpes' Snow Park and Slide zones

SLIDE
Boarder
Cross
Free
Cross

GRAND NORD / GRAND NORD BIS

The Grand Nord has the distinction of allowing the continuous descent from summit to base by providing the sole on-piste link out of the Toura 2600 area. It can therefore get very busy, particularly later in the afternoons. The route begins through a tunnel behind the Chalet de la Toura bar/restaurant, flowing out of the lower plain at Toura 2600. At the wide junction with the Gours blue ahead (see page 156), turn left. The route then flows as a wide, high-end blue straight down towards the Lac du Plan area, with a number of variations wide to the left, to merge with the Grand Nord Bis blue and the Tête Moute and Bellecombes reds. A more gentle escape track has also been cut into the hillside on the right to allow nervous novices to ease their way down the steeper upper pitch.

The Grand Nord Bis is a good variant begun higher to the left. It is reached at the end of the Liaison Super Diable a Toura link track (see page 134) and/or by riding to that point from the top of l'Envers button lift (40) from the Snow Park.

The entrance is to the left off the high ground overlooking the Chalet de la Toura bar/restaurant, on the final approach to the Jandri Express station, and is a wide lip on to this broad, high-end blue. The piste converges with the other routes sharing these slopes as described above for the prime Grand Nord. All routes finally blend and run as one through a chicane of speed-control barriers to schuss across the flat Lac du Plan area and link with the Bellecombes chair lift and/or to continue the descent via the Route de la Thuit green.

Another option is to peel off to the right at the point where you enter the Lac du Plan area to start the Route de la Fée blue, linking towards La Fée 2100.

ROUTE DE LA FÉE

A long and easy trail around the much quieter and wilder margins of the ski domain via La Fée 2100. It is accessed via the lower section of the Grand Nord blue, or any of the routes that merge with the Grand Nord (see opposite), by keeping high to the right as you emerge into the Lac du Plan area. The piste map gives the impression that the piste is descending down the valley, but on the ground it is actually traversing gently along the valley side. This start section is a long, flat skate until it rounds the front of the crag to sweep out wide to the right above La Fée 2100. This next section is much better, allowing you to traverse across to La Fée bar/restaurant (see page 185) furthest to the right, or to drop down to the left on to the fall-line and join the final sections of the Aymes black and the Fée red runs, on an often bumpy, mild red profile slope which funnels down to an easy link with La Fée chair-lift station (37) below left (see page 157).

La Fée bar/restaurant

The second half of the route bypasses La Fée chair lift and is joined from the right by traffic from the Gours blue. It then passes through some lovely peaceful scenery as a gentle trundle all the way to the base of the Voûte (31) and Thuit (32) chair lifts (see pages 121 and 132 respectively).

GOURS

A worthwhile excursion through a much quieter and wilder sector of the ski domain, beginning at a junction with the Grand Nord blue at Toura 2600, beyond the tunnel behind the Chalet de la Toura bar/restaurant; keep straight ahead for the Gours. An alternative start for more advanced-ability visitors is provided via the short Gours Bis black-graded link, only accessible from the Brêche red run (see page 173) when descending from the glacial zone.

The upper section of the Gours is an enjoyable cruise, swooping into a wide and peaceful cirque, with some really inviting freeride terrain off to the right. The piste funnels across a little bridge across a river gully, before continuing as an easy cruise sweeping down to the valley floor, requiring a skate to keep momentum along the flat shore of a frozen tarn – picnic spot here to the left. Once past this long, mid-section slog, the route picks up the pace again, twisting and turning with a mild red character down to a good link with La Fée chair lift (37). You can also bypass the lift to join the lower Route de la Fée blue (see page 157).

FREERIDE GULLY

Those of good intermediate ability or above could seek out the lovely little gully at the point where the Gours blue funnels across a small bridge (see above). Turn sharp left immediately after the bridge and ride/side-step up and over the high ground to get a good drop-in point. The gully is narrow and bumpy, with high side walls, boulder drop-offs and a tricky compression exiting out to rejoin the Gours piste on the valley floor.

LA FÉE CHAIR LIFT (37)

- 545 m (1788 ft) vertical rise
- 1815 m (1986 yd) long
- 2600 passengers/hour

The sole lift serving the often overlooked yet enjoyable La Fée sector, facilitating quick circuits on the rewarding terrain at this quieter side of the domain. The base station is an easy link from all pistes in this sector.

The journey up provides a good opportunity to check out the terrain on the Aymes black and Fée red routes below and to the sides of the lift line. On arrival, there is a picnic spot with a piste map/information post and tool point ahead right. U-turn right for the Aymes black, or turn sharp left for the Fée red. A drop-in point for the steep Sautet ungroomed black is ahead left by the fence. Ahead left too is a blue-graded ridge-run linking to the junction point of the Grand Nord and Gours blues at Toura 2600.

If this chair lift has closed when you reach it, do not panic! Join the Route de la Fée blue (see page 155) to traverse around to the base of the Voûte chair lift (31) (see page 121) and the Thuit chair lift (32) (see page 132). If they have also stopped, you can hike up the winding track cut into the Voûte red run to reach the Crêtes 2100 area interchange (see page 118).

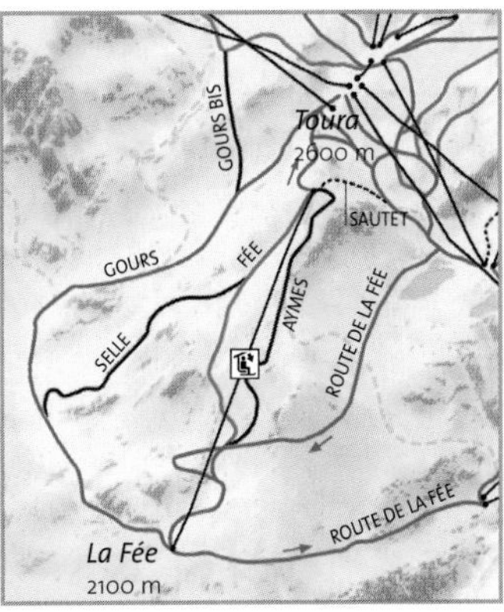

SAUTET

Short, and not often open, but a real gem when accessible. It is easy to miss on the local piste map – just a short dotted line off the arrival point of La Fée chair lift (37) (see previous page). The entrance is a gap in the fence on the summit ridge, roped off and closed if conditions are unstable. The views from this point are down over the Grand Nord blue and up the flanks of the Tête Moute towards the Toura 2600 area interchange ahead left, with the Lac du Plan area down to the right.

From the drop-in off the ridge you are immediately committed to a tough workout, free to choose any line down. The steep slope angle tops out at around 55 degrees. Exit on to the Grand Nord blue to either reach the Route de la Fée blue (see page 155) off to the right, or schuss straight across the flat Lac du Plan area towards the Bellecombes chair lift (see page 137) and/or the Route de la Thuit green (see page 130).

FÉE

A good red cruise, starting quickly off the arrival point of La Fée chair lift (37) (see previous page). After a good run in, the piste flattens into an easy, wide motorway, swinging to the left and skirting around the lip of a huge chute, which drops away steeply on the right-hand side and houses the Selle black run (see opposite). The lower half of the Fée piste runs down the line of La Fée chair lift as a mild-to-fair red with some testing terrain to the left towards the Aymes black run. La Fée bar/restaurant is easy to reach out to the right, midway down. Alternatively, keep straight down to merge with the Aymes black and Route de la Fée blue towards La Fée chair-lift station.

SELLE

A very good challenge for confident intermediates, accessed from the top section of the Fée red (see opposite). The run is housed in a huge, steep chute, off the right-hand edge of the Fée piste. The earlier you drop in the tougher the ride is, with a myriad different lines possible from anywhere along the rim. The descent then maintains a very consistent slope angle for the majority of the run, funnelling down towards the tarn area in the valley below. The route is designated as a groomed piste but is often left ungroomed after fresh snowfalls; it should definitely feature on your must-do list when that happens. The only drawback to this route is that it has a very flat finish across a tarn depression at the bottom of the run, requiring a hike out if the snow is deep and unpisted – the very time the run is at its most appealing. On exiting, you meet the flat mid-section of the Gours blue (see page 156) and join that to reach La Fée chair lift again.

A fair alternative to avoid the slog at the bottom is to play on the uppermost section and then traverse left to reach La Fée bar/restaurant before you go too low.

AYMES

Not long, and merely equivalent to a good red, but this decent run often gives the best ride at La Fée. The route starts as a wide and gentle blue-profile ridge run. It then spills down the spine of the mountain to develop a much more respectable slope angle, descending on the fall-line down the left-hand side of La Fée chair lift. The rocky inter-piste terrain to the right-hand side, under the lift line, is the most testing variant. The run finishes by joining the Route de la Fée blue to La Fée chair lift base.

GLACIER SKI SECTOR

Les Deux Alpes' signature ski sector is dominated by the twin pericline summits of the Dôme de la Lauze and Dôme de Puy Salié, the highest lift-accessible mountaintops in Isère. Unusually for such an extreme environment, it is easily accessible by both beginners and non-skiers. All skiers of at least confident novice ability should tackle the summit-to-base route at least once, from the top of the Dôme de la Lauze T-bar lift (52), down to the village of Mont-de-Lans, a non-stop on-piste descent of 2220 m (7282 ft). Visitors of intermediate standard should be sure not to miss the exciting and innovative Slide zones (see page 174), and this sector is also linked to the legendary off-piste Vallons de la Meije ski and mountaineering domain at La Grave, a truly awesome experience for visitors of more advanced abilities (see page 203).

JANDRI EXPRESS 2 CABLE CAR (56)

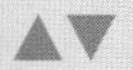

- 575 m (1887 ft) vertical rise
- 2640 m (2888 yd) long
- 1800 passengers/hour

The twin upper section of Les Deux Alpes' arterial declutchable cable car, departing from a mid-station shared with the Jandri Express 1 at the Toura 2600 area interchange, providing the final connection with the summit area of the ski domain. The circular cabins give a great perspective over this realm of rock, ice and permanent snow cover and the surrounding panorama of major Alpine peaks.

On arrival, exit to the right out on to the compact plateau at the Glacier 3200 area interchange (see over for orientation).

Les Deux Alpes' Glacier sector, accessible by all

GLACIERS CHAIR LIFT (42)

10¼ mins

- 600 m (1969 ft) vertical rise
- 2680 m (2932 yd) long
- 3430 passengers/hour

The 'gear-on' lift option to the glacial zone, allowing you to ski off on arrival and not waste a minute of skiing time. The lift base is tucked away on a ledge behind and below the level of Le Panoramic bar/restaurant, at the Toura 2600 area interchange. The get-on point is relatively easy to reach from the main lifts' level, via a short pisted access track (see page 146 for orientation). There is a tool point at the directional signs post on the final approach, along with clear sector-information boards.

The control gates are staggered; the four right-hand ones open slightly before the other four, so watch the gates and not the person beside you for your cue to advance. The chairs have well-padded seats and lumbar supports, making the open and exposed trip as pleasant as possible at this altitude. Advanced riders should study the steep and rocky couloirs below left, home to the Clot de Chalance and Couloir Electrique off-piste descents.

Five minutes into the journey, the lift comes to a mid-station. This is a get-on point only, accessible from the Brêche red piste – stay seated with the safety bar down. The chairs twist to the left before reconnecting with the haul cable for the upper part of the journey. The cluster of steep parallel chutes below and in the terrain ahead left at this point house the Slide zone modules.

On arrival at the Glacier 3200 area interchange, go straight ahead for the Roche-Mantel green piste; U-turn to the left to start the Serre Pallas blue and to reach the Dôme Express Funicular (54); or, turn to the right for the main interchange level (see opposite for orientation).

GLACIER 3200 AREA INTERCHANGE

This is the summit station interchange for Les Deux Alpes, topping off the series of interconnected lifts and services hubs. The main focus of activity here is at the huge Glaciers bar/restaurant complex (see page 188), an aircraft hanger-sized building plonked on a wide ledge at the tongue of the Glacier du Mont-de-Lans and just a flat amble/skate away from the upper station of the Jandri Express 2 cable car (56) (see page 161). As well as the cable car, the lift station also houses an interior picnic saloon, accessed via a piste-side lower ground floor door positioned under the arriving lift lines.

The building between the lift station and the restaurant complex is the main high-altitude piste/mountain patrol station, housing public WCs and a tool point with work benches for the ski-station personnel (ask permission first if you need to use the tools). This central area of the interchange has a piste map and directional sign post. The three-seater Roche-Mantel chair lift (43) (see page 171), serving the lower slopes on the adjacent Glacier de Mantel, arrives at the front of the interchange area. The gentle piste flowing away below left on the far side is the Roche-Mantel green piste (see page 170).

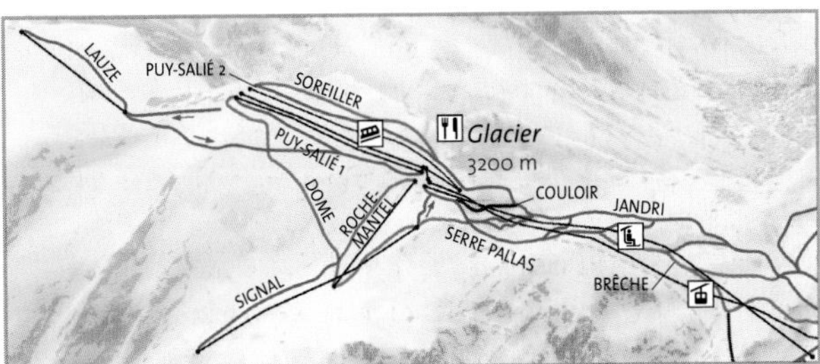

The main glacier slopes flow down to the edge of the interchange area, parallel to the twin Puy-Salié T-bar lifts (47 and 48) (see page 167), which are based in front of the Glaciers bar/restaurant. The pistes are, from left to right looking up, the Puy-Salié 1 and Puy-Salié 2 blues and the Soreiller green.

The Glaciers chair lift (42) arrives at the far side of the Jandri Express station, furthest away from the Glaciers bar/restaurant, requiring a stroll or a skate to reach the restaurant and the glacier slopes T-bar lifts. The piste to the left of the arrival point of the Glaciers chair lift is the Serre Pallas blue (see page 173), which heads towards the Slide zones and the Toura 2600 interchange.

The wide slope flowing off the interchange area and veering left down the gentle face of the mountain is a blue-graded link piste towards the lower station of the Dôme Express funicular (54) (see page 166), based 100 m (328 ft) below the main interchange. There is also an inclined-rail elevator at the funicular station, L'Ascenseur (53) (see opposite), connecting the funicular station with the Glaciers bar/restaurant complex.

Glaciers bar/restaurant complex at the Glaciers 3200 area interchange

CAUTION

You are now on a glacier, where dangerous crevasses are numerous even if you cannot see them. The piste patrol have clearly marked out the pistes and footpaths and you are strongly advised to stay on them.

If you take off your skis or board, you become simply an unroped pedestrian in a serious mountaineering environment, so keep your gear on at all times when moving around on the glaciers.

Walkers are strictly forbidden to go on the glaciers!

L'ASCENSEUR (53)

- 65 m (213 ft) vertical rise
- 90 m (99 yd) long
- 600 passengers/hour

Because the Dôme Express funicular station is located around 200 m (219 yd) away from, and 100 m (328 ft) below, the main Glaciers 3200 area interchange, this elevator provides the link between the two levels. The upper access point is located just below the Glaciers bar/restaurant building, which is accessible either at the far corner of the main restaurant interior, or piste-side externally at the lower end of the building, facing the cable car station.

The elevator cabin travels externally on an inclined rail. The bright cabin is glazed at the front and gives good views over the lower glacier area towards Toura 2600. At the lower level, follow the signs down the stairs past the piste-level exit/entrance to reach the underground funicular station.

DÔME EXPRESS FUNICULAR (54)

3¾ mins ▲▼

- 325 m (1066 ft) vertical rise
- 1700 m (1860 yd) long
- 1500 passengers/hour

One of the world's highest-altitude tube trains, climbing to 3400 m (11,152 ft), just under the summit of the Dôme de Puy-Salié. The train is accessible to skiers and non-skiers. As well as serving the highest altitude pistes, it provides access to Les Deux Alpes' wonderful Grotte de Glace (Ice Cave, see page 189) and reaches one of the most stunning viewpoints in the Alps.

The funicular's lower station is located around 200 m (219 yd) away from, and 100 m (328 ft) below, the main Glaciers 3200 area interchange. To reach it, either take L'Ascenseur elevator (53) (see previous page) from the Glaciers bar/restaurant complex, or ski down using the short, blue-graded access pistes. Steps lead down to the platforms, passing through a small holding area controlled by traffic lights; once on the platforms you can board the train from either side. The carriage floor slopes slightly forward, but becomes level as the train climbs the inclined track. There are no seats, but plenty of leaning posts.

On arrival at the top, take the stairs at the top end of the inclined platform. There are then three standard elevators; each holds 27 passengers and takes one minute to reach the surface. There is a tool point and work bench just before the automatic doors at the final exit. Outside, the Grotte de Glace is just ahead; the viewpoint and principal glacier pistes are beyond this. Keep left for the Soreiller green, Puy-Salié 2 blue and viewpoint orientation table. Go right under the T-bar lift's anchor pylon cables to link with the Dôme de la Lauze T-bar lift (52) to the summit and to link with La Grave.

PUY-SALIÉ T-BAR LIFTS (47 & 48)

7½ mins

- 265 m (870 ft) vertical rise
- 1580 m (1729 yd) long
- 1200 passengers/hour x 2

Departing from directly in front of the Glaciers bar/restaurant at the Glacier 3200 area interchange, these twin T-bars are the principal surface lifts serving the prime glacier pistes; long queues here are common. The two lifts share the same pylons and run side by side.

On arrival, turn right for the Grotte de Glace, the viewpoint orientation table and the Soreiller green and the Puy-Salié 2 blue pistes; or go ahead left on the flat access track to link with the Dôme de la Lauze T-bar lift (52) to the summit and towards La Grave; or U-turn left for the Puy-Salié 1 blue and Dôme red pistes.

DÔME DE LA LAUZE T-BAR LIFT (52)

3¾ mins

- 140 m (459 ft) vertical rise
- 760 m (831 yd) long
- 1200 passengers/hour

The summit ski lift, reaching the highest lift-accessible point in Les Deux Alpes' ski domain and allowing the onward link towards La Grave's incredible Vallons de la Meije off-piste realm (see page 168). The lift is positioned a couple of hundred metres away from the Puy-Salié 1 and 2 T-bar lifts and the Dôme Express funicular upper station; a flat 2-way pisted access track connects them.

The piste running down parallel to your right as you ascend on this lift is the Lauze blue, Les Deux Alpes' highest altitude piste. On arrival, U-turn right to start the Lauze blue, or go straight ahead to access La Grave's ski area (see page 168 for link) or to reach the summit of the Dôme de la Lauze.

LA GRAVE LINK

Not all ski passes permit access to La Grave, so check with the ski pass office before setting out.

From the top of the Dôme de la Lauze T-bar lift (52), you can reach La Grave's ski area in one of two ways: either towed behind the station's tracked vehicle link (weekdays only and limited to a maximum of 500 passengers per day), or by trekking/skating along the pisted track across the wide summit ridge. On reaching the arrival point of La Grave's La Girose button lift, take the well-marked blue piste down the right-hand side of the lift line, running past the get-on point and straight across the glacier towards the base of the Trifides button lift ahead left. The Haut Dessus bar/restaurant (see page 213) and La Meije cable car station are then just below left along a pisted ridge track.

(!) Warning – although the link to La Grave's glacier blue pistes is reasonably straightforward and accessible to all visitors of at least competent novice standard, the surrounding Vallons de la Meije domain is totally off-piste and is strictly for advanced riders/mountaineers only, preferably accompanied by a qualified mountain guide (see La Grave section starting on page 203).

(!) The return link-lifts close quite early and can close completely and unexpectedly if weather conditions deteriorate (see page 208 for return links). The only means of escape is to go down to La Grave village using La Meije cable car. The only way back to Les Deux Alpes from La Grave is an expensive 26 km/16¼ mile taxi ride.

Stunning vistas from the summit of the Dôme de la Lauze

LAUZE

A huge, icy motorway with one of the most commanding views in the Alps. The piste is a decent blue and flows straight down the glacier parallel to the Dôme de la Lauze T-bar lift line. At the bottom, schuss to the right to reach the get-on point for that lift, or continue straight on, veering ahead right on the wide, flat track, to link towards Les Deux Alpes' Dôme red and Puy-Salié 1 blue pistes.

PUY-SALIÉ 1 & 2

These twin runway-wide pistes are the busy principal slopes in the glacier ski area. They run down either side of their namesake twin T-bar lifts, directly towards the Glacier 3200 area interchange. The Puy-Salié 2 piste to the far left runs next to the Soreiller green piste and links to the Jandri blue for the full summit-to-base route. The Puy-Salié 1 piste descends to the right and links with the Roche-Mantel green piste (see page 170) to the lower glacier runs.

DÔME

Easily the best intermediate-level piste on the glaciers, beginning from the top of the Puy-Salié 1 and 2 T-bar lifts (47 and 48) and the Dôme Express funicular (54). The uppermost section is quite mild, crossing a link track coming from the Lauze blue piste and then taking the fall-line on the massively wide and surprisingly steep Glacier de Mantel, giving a good workout in the thin air. The Echine des Chèvres off-piste route is immediately to the right on the far side of the boundary rope. Warning! This looks deceptively similar to the Dôme piste, but it is an unprotected crevasse zone and you should enter only with a qualified mountain guide.

The Dôme piste maintains a consistently good slope angle, flowing out to join the lower section of the Roche-Mantel green. Traverse straight ahead to join the green route towards the Roche-Mantel chair lift (43) or, for the best link, swoop down to the right to make the imperceptible transition on to the milder Signal blue towards the Signal chair lift (45).

ROCHE-MANTEL

Really a blue piste, giving confident learners a frisson of excitement since it is a little more involved than the bland motorway of the Soreiller green piste. It begins at the Glacier 3200 area interchange beside the three-seater Roche-Mantel chair lift (43) and arcs down on to a wide and gently undulating glacier slope. Midway down, signs direct you to the left and on to a contour-line track, under the lines of the Signal chair lift towards the get-on point for the Roche-Mantel chair lift. Another option is to continue straight down, flowing seamlessly into the only slightly steeper Signal blue piste to reach the Signal chair lift (45).

ROCHE-MANTEL CHAIR LIFT (43)

7½ mins

- 150 m (492 ft) vertical rise
- 955 m (1045 yd) long
- 1160 passengers/hour

Caution: there are no foot rests on the safety bar on this chair lift. It is reached via an access track from the Roche-Mantel green and is also accessible from the Dôme red.

On arrival at the top, the Puy-Salié 1 T-bar lift is ahead left. The Glaciers bar/restaurant complex is ahead right and the Jandri Express 2 cable car station is to the right. Skate past the cable car station to begin the blue-graded link piste down to the Dôme Express funicular station (see page 166) and/or to link with the Jandri blue piste (see page 172) for the onward descent towards Les Deux Alpes via the Toura 2600 area interchange; or, U-turn left for the Roche-Mantel green piste.

SIGNAL CHAIR LIFT (45)

5 mins

- 350 m (1148 ft) vertical rise
- 1275 m (1395 yd) long
- 2000 passengers/hour

Based at the lowest piste-accessible point on the glacier, at the bottom of the Signal blue piste. The lift arrives on top of a crag a few hundred metres away from the Glacier 3200 area interchange: go ahead left for a blue-graded link towards the Dôme Express funicular (54) and L'Ascenseur elevator (53). This route also links with the Serre Pallas (see page 173) and Jandri blue (see page 172) in the direction of Les Deux Alpes. Alternatively, veer ahead right for the short Envers du Signal red link to the Serre Pallas blue. U-turning to the left on arrival drops on to a short but steep red run down to the base of the Roche-Mantel chair lift (43).

JANDRI

This long, high-end blue provides a vital seamless link between the glacier pistes and Toura 2600, enabling a summit-to-base descent (see pages 176–9 for full route-finders). It gives a varied and enjoyable cruise through rocky, sub-glacial terrain at the narrowest section of the ski domain.

The run begins as a continuation of the Puy-Salié 2 blue piste at the tongue of the glacier, to the left of the Glaciers bar/ restaurant when descending, serving as a good link to the Dôme Express funicular (54). Passing the funicular station, the route then presents two options: ahead right is a short, direct red-graded variation; the main blue-graded route continues wide to the left. Both routes converge below and become a gentle green-profile cruise.

The mid-section then becomes more demanding: steeper, bumpier and normally choppier because of the heavy daily traffic flow on this busy arterial route. This section is a challenge for novices, but is wide enough to be manageable. Les Deux Alpes' enjoyable Slide zones cover the gnarly terrain above right and their exit points run out to meet the Jandri in a series of junctions all the way through this section.

The lower section is a standard blue motorway, spilling on to the flat floor of the big snowbowl at the Toura 2600 area interchange (see page 148 for orientation). A better option is to keep high to either the left or the right: to the left gives the best link with the Snow Park chair lifts; to the right you can join the Brêche red to bypass the flat snowbowl floor for a fair link with the Glaciers chair lift (42) (see page 162), the Gours blue (see page 156) and the Grand Nord blue (see page 154). The latter option is the one to take for the summit-to-base route.

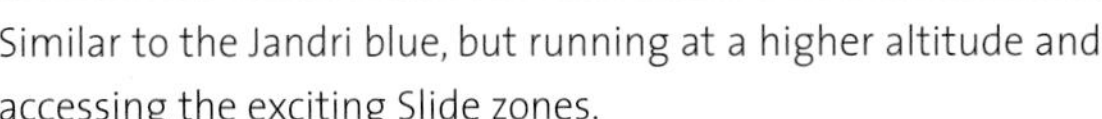

SERRE PALLAS

Similar to the Jandri blue, but running at a higher altitude and accessing the exciting Slide zones.

The route begins at the arrival point of the Glaciers chair lift (42) at the Glacier 3200 area interchange. All junctions leaving the Serre Pallas are to the left. The first is a link to the Dôme Express funicular (54), followed in turn by the entrances to each of the Slide features (see pages 174–5), alongside various straightforward links down to the Jandri blue. The Serre Pallas finishes by swinging left to merge with the Jandri piste. The two entrances for the Brêche red are to the right just above that point.

BRÊCHE

Reached via the Serre Pallas blue, this fair red accesses the final two Slide zones (see pages 174–5) plus a handy bypass around the Toura 2600 area interchange. There are two entrances: the higher one links with the mid-station of the Glaciers chair lift (42) – although this provides little advantage. The 'Cascades' Slide feature drops off to the left just where the upper Brêche variation descends steeply to join the lower one; the 'Corniche' Slide feature is then just a little further along. Continuing on the Brêche, there is a short, steep blast to the left to join the Jandri piste finishing close to the Snow Park. Alternatively, stay high to the right for the Gours Bis black link to the Gours blue (see page 156).

The Brêche finishes after a short, steep pitch above the plain at Toura 2600. Swing high to the right and run over the top of the tunnel near the Chalet de la Toura bar/restaurant to link with the Upper Toura 2600 Level lift stations (see page 146) and the Gours and Grand Nord blues (see page 154 for latter).

SLIDE ZONES

A truly laudable effort by the station to harness the wilder, normally off-piste-only gullies and chutes in the otherwise barren and narrow strip of sub-glacial terrain between the Glacier 3200 and Toura 2600 areas, opening them up as freestyle features. They are great fun and should definitely feature on the 'must-do' list for visitors of intermediate standard and above.

The zones are accessed by the Serre Pallas blue and Brêche red pistes (see previous page), and are served by the Jandri Express 2 cable car (56) and the Glaciers chair lift (42), the chair lift making it possible to ride in 'gear-on' circuits. All of the features exit on to the Jandri blue piste, which is then used for the onward link back towards the Toura 2600 area interchange (see previous page for route description).

The four different Slide zones are the Couloir, the Canyons, the Cascades and the Corniches.

COULOIR

The first of the Slide features accessed from the Serre Pallas blue, at an altitude of 3100 m (10,168 ft):

- A 150 m (164 yd) straight chute, with a 35 degree slope angle, which can be tackled at full tilt.

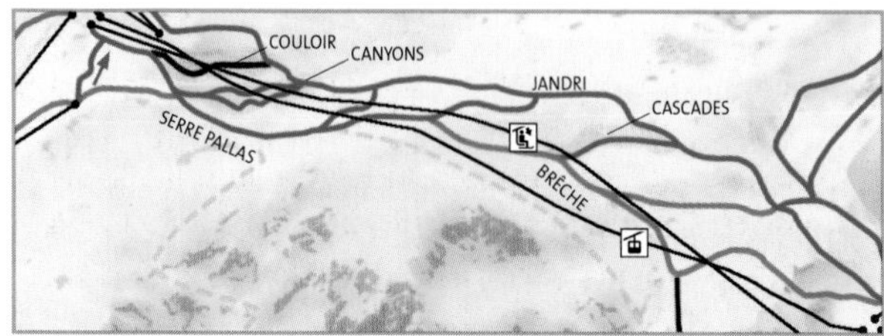

CANYONS

The second of the Slide features accessed from the Serre Pallas blue, at an altitude of 3000 m (9840 ft):

- Two parallel freeform Boarder/SkierCross courses. The left-hand run is the steepest, the right-hand one has a couple of meandering variations and contains a 'Corniche' feature (see below).

CASCADES

The first of the Slide features accessed from the Brêche red, at an altitude of 2800 m (9184 ft):

- Two parallel runs with at least five in-line stepped kickers each, great for duels with a buddy.

CORNICHES

There are two 'Corniche' modules, the first off the Serre Pallas blue and contained within the 'Canyons' zone at an altitude of 3000 m (9840 ft), the second standing on its own and accessed from the Brêche red, at an altitude of 2800 m (9184 ft):

- Basically two big wedge-shaped ledges, offering drops-offs ranging from 1–5 m ($3\frac{1}{4}$–$16\frac{1}{2}$ ft).

JUMP TRAINING

A great facility for safely working your way up to more daring freestyle antics in the Slide zones and Snow Park, consisting of a Big Air ramp launching off to land in a huge air-bag crash mat. Based on the town slopes at Les Deux Alpes, just in front of the Jandri 1 gondola (the 'white eggs'). Included at no extra cost on all ski passes and open to all responsible users.

POINT-TO-POINT ROUTES: COMPETENT NOVICES

PIED MOUTET SECTOR » CRÊTES 2100 AREA INTERCHANGE

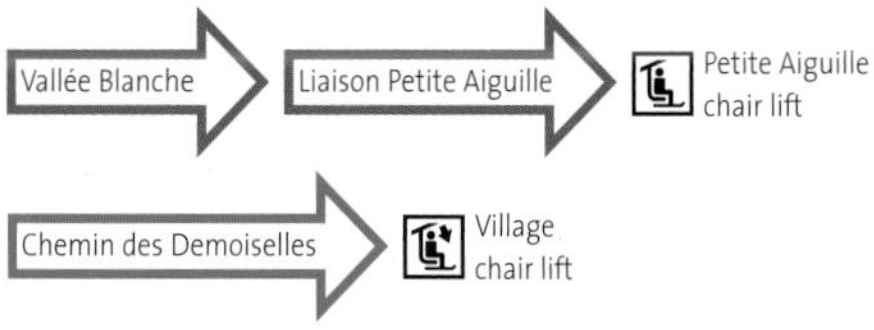

LES 2 ALPES 1800 » DIABLE 2400 AREA INTERCHANGE

LES DEUX ALPES (MONT-DE-LANS QUARTER) » DIABLE 2400 AREA INTERCHANGE

LES DEUX ALPES (VENOSC QUARTER) » CRÊTES 2100 AREA INTERCHANGE

DIABLE 2400 AREA INTERCHANGE » LES DEUX ALPES (VIA CRÊTES 2100 AREA INTERCHANGE)

LES DEUX ALPES (MONT-DE-LANS QUARTER) » TOURA 2600 AREA INTERCHANGE

LES DEUX ALPES (VENOSC QUARTER) » TOURA 2600 AREA INTERCHANGE

LES DEUX ALPES » SNOW PARK

SNOW PARK » LES DEUX ALPES

LES DEUX ALPES » DÔME DE LA LAUZE (SUMMIT)

DÔME DE LA LAUZE (SUMMIT) » LES DEUX ALPES

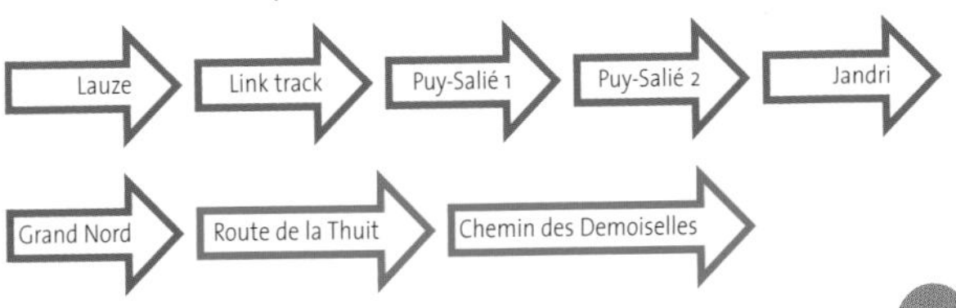

POINT-TO-POINT ROUTES: GOOD INTERMEDIATES AND ABOVE

PIED MOUTET SECTOR » CRÊTES 2100 AREA INTERCHANGE

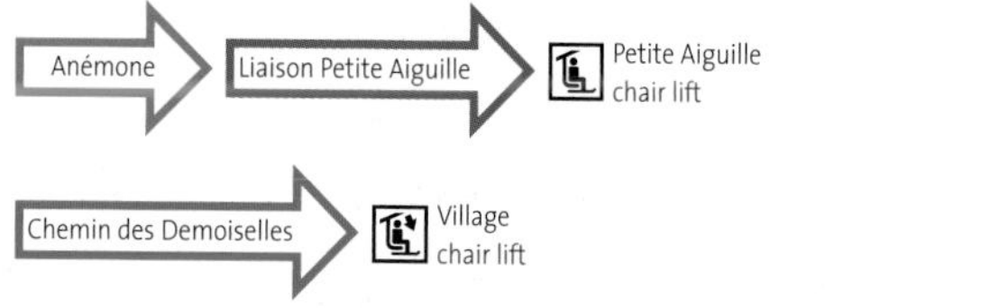

LES 2 ALPES 1800 » DIABLE 2400 AREA INTERCHANGE

LES DEUX ALPES (MONT-DE-LANS QUARTER) » DIABLE 2400 AREA INTERCHANGE

DIABLE 2400 AREA INTERCHANGE » LES DEUX ALPES

LES DEUX ALPES (VENOSC QUARTER) » CRÊTES 2100 AREA INTERCHANGE

LES DEUX ALPES (MONT-DE-LANS QUARTER) » TOURA 2600 AREA INTERCHANGE

LES DEUX ALPES (VENOSC QUARTER) » TOURA 2600 AREA INTERCHANGE

SNOW PARK » LES DEUX ALPES

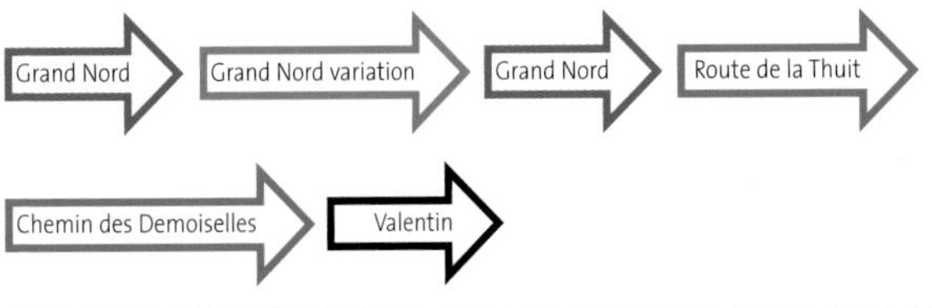

DÔME DE LA LAUZE (SUMMIT) » MONT-DE-LANS VILLAGE

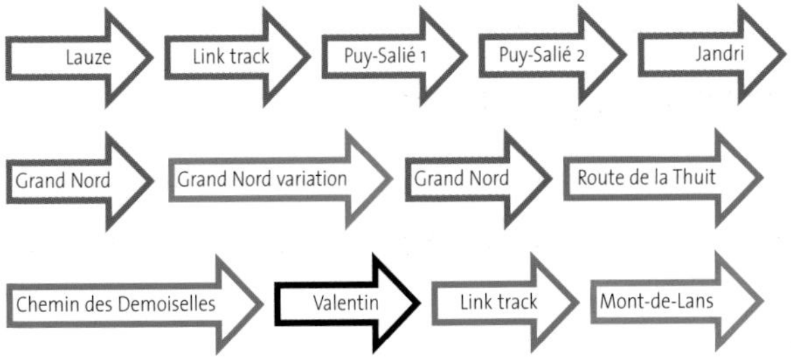

Le Diable au Cœur

MOUNTAIN BARS & RESTAURANTS

As expected for such a well-established ski area, there are a good number of on-piste bars and restaurants, well spaced throughout the domain so that you are never far away from a refuelling and refreshment point. Some offer a self-service food selection, but the majority are à la carte. Most are large and bustling venues at the busy lift and piste interchanges, but the station has made an effort to ensure that these present a service based on traditional styles. Additionally, there are a couple of more authentic Oisans mountain restaurants, where the fare on offer is centred on good-quality classic regional dishes and where the ambiance is warm and the service is personal.

All provide a full catering service from around 11.30–15.00 hours. All also provide a full bar and snacks service all day. Almost all have public WCs, some of which are serviced and levy a small charge.

All of the venues except the one at La Fée can be reached by non-skiers, using one of the many ski lifts which are accessible to pedestrians holding a Pedestrian Pass (see page 76).

LES DEUX ALPES BASE

Because the resort of Les Deux Alpes is so large, the number and variety of bars and restaurants easily accessible from the town slopes is immense. The town slopes by the ice rink and swimming pool have the most piste-side venues. The Grand Place at Les 2 Alpes 1800 is also easy to ride to on-piste and has a handful of busy bars and restaurants; it also houses the closest supermarket to the pistes. Unlike the on-mountain venues, most of the restaurants in town serve lunch between 12.00 and 14.00 hours only.

◀ *Terrace at Le Diable au Cœur, Toura 2400*

PIED MOUTET SECTOR

This relatively quiet and more detached sector is not really representative of the ski domain as a whole. It has just the three on-mountain venues, one of which is quite remote from the main ski area. The two principal venues are much smaller than those found in the core ski area and offer a much more traditional mountain refuge atmosphere.

La Troïka €+ A plain but attractive wood-built cabin in a commanding position at the highest point on the Pied Moutet ridge, just above the Super Venosc chair lift (21) arrival point and close to the arrival point of the Pied Moutet chair lift (20). Compact south-facing terraces on two levels, overlooking the Vénéon Valley directly towards the Aiguille de Venosc and La Muzelle, with views across Les Deux Alpes to the core ski area. The lower terrace has deckchairs and the upper terrace has wooden bench tables and seating for food service. The cosy, wood-clad interior has a small bar and dining saloon. Food service is basic but adequate, focused on a range of tagliatelles and crêpes, with salads, grilled steak and sausage and chips also available. A very pleasant, unpretentious venue. No WCs on-site, but available nearby at the Super Venosc lift operator's cabin. t +33 (0)4 76 80 24 13

La Molière €+ Quite remote from the main ski area, way out in the woods past the Bons chair lift (18) and reached via the Nordic ski and snowshoeing circuit. Very tranquil surroundings, with views down the Romanche Valley towards le Bourg-d'Oisans. Limited opening hours and really only viable for cross-country skiers and walkers. Very basic food service, centred on a daily special and snacks; limited bar service.

La Bergerie Kanata €+ Definitely the most atmospheric and authentic venue in the domain, housed in a converted barn in the midst of this sector's principal Vallée Blanche slopes.

Very chilled ambiance, gentle music and deckchairs on a wide terrace, with plenty of bench-style tables and seating. The cosy interior is rustically decorated and centred around a raised open fireplace. Food ranges from standard snacks to wholesome regional specialities including tartiflette; fresh mussels, chips and beer at a special all-in price every Friday. Full bar service.

This location is easily reached on foot by following the way-marked snowshoe trail from the base of the slopes at the edge of the resort. Guided nighttime snowshoe excursions including dinner are a regular feature – enquire at the central tourist office.

The Kanata is also renown for its igloo 'village' – overnight stays in the igloos are possible, with dinner, sleeping bags and breakfast included in the price. ⓣ +33 (0)6 12 29 49 03

Igloo at La Bergerie Kanata

CRÊTES/DIABLE SECTORS

The bustling Crêtes 2100 and Diable 2400 area interchanges, on the skyline ridge above Les Deux Alpes, each house large and popular restaurants which are the main focal points at these busy lift and piste hubs. The one at Diable 2400 is possibly the best quality in the entire domain.

La Patache €€ Large, split-level chalet in the middle of the Crêtes 2100 area interchange; one of the station's original mountain restaurants, on this site for over 30 years. A large, south-facing terrace juts out at the front on raised supports. Beneath, there is a little snack bar on a small piste-side veranda, offering hot drinks and a basic bar service, plus hot dogs, chips, pizza slices and filled baguettes (interior picnic saloon here too).

The main restaurant is self-service. The interior is bright and reasonably attractive and the food is good by self-service standards: fresh salads, regional charcuterie, pasta, grilled meats, tartiflette and a decent range of homemade pastries and desserts. On the terrace, there are dining tables and deckchairs; waiter service for drinks only. On request, the bar supplies chains and padlocks to lock your equipment.

Le Diable au Cœur €€+ A high-quality venue in a great position on the shoulder of the ridge at Diable 2400, giving a stunning view over the Vénéon Valley. Located right next to the Diable gondola lift (23) upper station. Housed in a lovely big wooden chalet with a large, cantilevered terrace wrapping around the south-facing front of the restaurant. There are deckchairs piste-side at the entrance and on the terrace, which is furnished with bistro-style tables and chairs. Full table service for food and drinks.

The interior is decorated to a high standard. There is a reception area with maitre d' service at the main entrance. Newpapers and magazines are available and hangers are provided for wet jackets. There are gear racks by the main entrance, which are lockable if you bring your own padlock.

Food on offer is focused around good-quality regional specialities, plus a refined range of salads and grilled meats. The restaurant also opens regularly in the evenings, organizing 'after hours' gondola lift transport, dinner and a torchlit descent back to town. ⓣ +33 (0)4 76 79 99 50 ⓦ www.lediableaucoeur.com

TOURA/LA FÉE SECTORS

There are three establishments in these intertwined core sectors: two large and bustling venues at the busy Toura 2600 area interchange, plus a smaller, more laid-back operation in more peaceful surroundings just above La Fée 2100.

Chalet de la Fée €+ Tucked away in the quieter La Fée sector, well away from the crowds, the 'chalet' is positioned near the confluence point of the Route de la Fée blue, Fée red and Aymes black runs, above La Fée chair lift base.

The piste-side terrace has waiter service for both food and drinks, it gives a good vantage point to study the off-piste routes in the Clot de Chalance and has great views out over the Romanche Valley towards Alpe d'Huez in the distance. The two-floor interior bar and restaurant is plain but welcoming.

Fare on offer revolves around an unpretentious snack menu: soups, burgers and chips, omelette and chips, etc., supplemented with pasta and grilled meats; ideal if you want an unfussy refuelling stop. ⓣ +33 (0)4 76 80 24 13

Chalet de la Toura €€+ Huge log cabin on the lower plain at the Toura 2600, acting as the busy social hub for the core ski area and providing the closest catering to the Snow Park.

There is a snack-bar kiosk at the rear of the building serving the snow patio, and a cosy interior café-bar space with full bar service and snacks, including chips, hamburgers and filled baguettes. A large terrace at the front faces across the plain directly towards the Snow Park. One section is set out with deckchairs and has waiter service for drinks and snacks, the other is the main exterior dining area. An efficient meet-and-greet service controls access to the main terrace – the maitre d' will show you to the first available table and will get one of the team to take your order swiftly.

Inside, there is a cosy little bar to the left next to an open wood-fired pizza kitchen. The main interior dining saloon is roomy but has a cosy and homely feel, with quality decor and an open fire. There is table service throughout for both drinks and food.

The venue offers good-quality, wholesome meals: a fair range of salads, omelettes and grills, along with an excellent range of hand-thrown, wood-fired pizzas. ⓣ +33 (0)4 76 79 20 96

Le Panoramic €€ On the upper level at Toura 2600, close to the cable car stations, this is an attractive traditional chalet with an elevated south-facing terrace giving sweeping vistas over the Grand Nord area towards the summit of Tête Moute. A nice touch is the free-of-charge, staffed, backpack/equipment storage service just inside the main piste-side entrance at the bottom of the stairs up to the main bar/restaurant.

The venue offers both self-service and à la carte service; the main self-service dining saloon is quite plain and rustic, but airy and bright. The segregated à la carte dining area at the far side of the interior is more polished. There is also a separate crêpes service point in the middle of the main saloon and a microwave for public use.

The fair-sized terrace has deckchairs and bench tables and seating with waiter service for drinks, alongside a separate à la carte section furnished with individual tables and chairs.

Crêpes made to order at Le Panoramic

The self-service selection offers a limited range of ready-made salads and hot dishes, mostly pasta or meat and vegetable combos, tarts and desserts, canned and bottled drinks; wine is available in good-value pichets. The à la carte fare is hearty and wholesome, focused on regional specialities such as tartiflette and raviolis, along with a fair choice of select meat dishes and salads, finished off with a very tempting selection of homemade tarts and sweets. +33 (0)4 76 79 06 75

GLACIER SECTOR

There is only one catering site in the highest reaches of the ski domain, but it is the biggest in the domain. It is conveniently sited next to the Jandri Express 2 cable car station at the Glacier 3200 area interchange, at the base of the principal glacier pistes, allowing skiers and non-skiers alike to share in the amazing experience of being in this icy realm of permanent snow.

Les Glaciers €€ A massive, hanger-sized structure plonked on a wide ledge at the edge of the glacier at 3200 m (10,496 ft). The building is not attractive, but is functional and warm. There is a snack bar serving hot drinks, chips, hot dogs, burgers, etc., with a patio area overlooking the T-bar lifts get-on points. The far side of the building has a huge, south-facing terrace with plenty of tables, chairs and deckchairs. Lockable ski racks are available; they operate with tokens from the nearby token-vending machine.

Inside, there is a fully serviced bar and two separate restaurants: a self-service canteen and a segregated à la carte saloon. The main canteen is busy and brash, but the space is bright and roomy and the food selection is wide, with readymade salads and a choice of around 10 hot dishes, including pastas and meat and vegetable combos. Microwaves are available for public use.

Contained within this same area, but separated from it, is the à la carte dining area, which has been decorated in faux chalet style to give a slightly more refined experience. It offers more select variations of the main restaurant menu, including fair value set menus. +33 (0)4 76 79 21 36

Grotte de Glace at the summit of the Dôme de Puy-Salié

ALTERNATIVE ACTIVITIES

Les Deux Alpes is marketed as a high-energy, high-altitude mountain station, accessible to everyone. To this end, the station also provides a good range of activities and attractions to complement the principal snowsports. Full details and bookings from the central tourist office (Maison des 2 Alpes) at place des 2 Alpes in the middle of the resort. ☎ +33 (0)4 76 79 22 00

❗ Activities may not be covered by travel insurance (see page 52).

GROTTE DE GLACE (ICE CAVE)

A wonderful attraction for all visitors, easily accessible at the top of the Dôme Express funicular (54) on the summit of the Dôme de Puy-Salié at 3245 m (10,644 ft). The cave was dug out by hand and burrows 30 m (98 ft) down into the ancient ice of the Roche-Mantel glacier. Inside, artists have created chambers filled with huge ephemeral sculptures, including dinosaurs and tableaux depicting mountain life, backlit to glow eerily in the muted light. Small entrance charge; open daily 10.00–16.00 hours.

NON-SKIERS

A ski pass is not always necessary to participate in the alternative activities on offer – please enquire at the time of booking. Many ski lifts are accessible to foot passengers, but you will need a Pedestrian Pass to use them (see page 76). These passes additionally include one visit to the ice cave and the ice rink and two to the open-air swimming pool.

The villages of Mont-de-Lans and Venosc are accessible by ski lift and are included on all Pedestrian Pass options.

LA CROISIÈRE BLANCHE (THE WHITE CRUISE)

Another glacier attraction accessible to all visitors and a great way for non-skiers to discover the amazing glacial landscape on the roof of the Alps. The cruise is on board an adapted piste-basher, which trundles along the ridge to the summit of the Dôme de la Lauze at 3568 m (11,703 ft), slightly higher than the uppermost ski lift. Available on its own or as part of an inclusive package including lifts and entry to the Grotte de Glace (ice cave).

NORDIC SKIING / LANGLAUF

Downhill skiing and 'new-school' snowsports are the prime focus at Les Deux Alpes. Nordic skiing, or 'langlauf' ('ski du fond' in French), is not well catered for by the station. There is one compact pisted circuit on the lip of the Vénéon Valley near the Rivets button lift (16) and another more substantial and interesting trail into the Bons birch woods. It departs from the base of the Vallée Blanche chair lift (19) and is accessible from the pisted footbridge over the main road at the resort entrance. Ski passes are not required and the routes are open to all responsible users. An attractive itinerary is also marked out along the peaceful wooded valley beside the Vénéon River. This is accessible using the Venosc gondola lift (17) – round-trip passes are available directly from the gondola station.

Equipment hire is available from all good Alpine ski-rental shops in resort; the larger ski schools offer Nordic ski tuition.

SNOWSHOEING

Modern showshoes are made of lightweight materials and are very easy to master. They work by spreading your weight over a wider surface area, allowing you to walk more easily over snow, using a pair of ski poles for balance.

Referred to locally as *raquettes*, snowshoes provide a great way for all visitors to get out into the more tranquil corners of the mountains, where you are more likely to spot Alpine wildlife than you would in populated areas. Follow the waymarked snowshoe route in the Pied Moutet sector or hire a guide and head off into the wilds. Evening excursions under the stars are also available, including dinner at the atmospheric venue La Bergerie Kanata (see page 183). Equipment hire is available at most good ski-rental shops.

ICE SKATING

Les Deux Alpes has an Olympic-size outdoor ice rink, located next to the swimming pool on the rue des Sagnes, close to the place des 2 Alpes. This great facility is a real focal point at this part of the resort. It is open to the sky and the views and overlooked by the piste-side bars at the base of the central town slopes.

The ice rink is free for all holders of current Super Ski passes of at least six days' duration; otherwise there is a small admission charge payable. Skate hire is available on site, although there is a small extra charge for these for all users. Open daily 10.30–12.00, 15.00–18.30, and 20.30–23.00 hours (but not open for skating during Ice Glider hours, see below).

ICE GLIDERS

This is a really unusual activity and great fun for all. Basically, these are bumper cars on ice, powered by car batteries. You are free to bump and bash exactly as you would at a fairground. The activity is available at the resort's ice rink (see above) Open Tues 15.15–17.30 hours and Mon & Wed 20.45–22.30 hours, weather permitting. Small charge payable per person.

SNOWMOBILES

This thrilling motorsport is consistently the most requested alternative wintersports activity. Unlike the more usual closed circuits available in many other ski resorts, in Les Deux Alpes you can get out into the mountains and actually drive all the way up to Toura 2600 after the ski area has closed for the evening (accompanied by a guide), a round trip of almost 25 km (15½ miles). Each snowmobile can carry two people – drive the machine yourself or hang on tight as a passenger. Participants must be over 18 and anyone wishing to drive must hold a car driving licence. Find the information hut on the central town slopes, close to the Jandri lifts base stations. Ⓦ www.2alpesmotoneige.com

4 x 4 quad-bikes x 4 different sizes

QUADS

Head for the hills and ride off into the sunset on an all-terrain quad-motorbike, (accompanied by a guide), after the ski area has closed for the evening. As with the snowmobile excursions, you can drive all the way up to Toura 2600. The machines have automatic gearboxes and are great fun to handle. A driving licence is required. There is also a children's quad circuit at the base of the town slopes near the hotel Côte Brune (see town plan on page 65). Open all day, for children over 4 years of age, with 4 sizes of machine available; helmets provided. Ⓦ www.quad2alpes.com

ICE CLIMBING

An amazing adventure sport sure to appeal to all adrenaline junkies. A mountain guide teaches you the basics of climbing with ice axes and crampons and then you get to scale an incredible frozen waterfall. Bookings available through the Bureau des Guides (see page 76 for contact details).

FLYING

The Alps are even more breathtaking when seen from a bird's-eye viewpoint and Les Deux Alpes offers a couple of great ways to take to the air:

Helicopter Heli-skiing off summits is banned in France, but you can arrange for round-trip helicopter connections with Alpe d'Huez to ski in the huge Grandes Rousses ski domain or book an excursion to Italy where heli-skiing is permitted. Sightseeing trips over the Ecrins National Park and transfers to and from the airport are also possible. SAF Hélicoptères ⓣ +33 (0)4 76 79 75 01 ⓦ www.saf-helico.com

Paraglider Launch off into space above the deep and beautiful Vénéon Valley from the station's permanent paragliding launch site at Diable 2400. You will be harnessed into a steerable paragliding canopy in tandem with a professional pilot, experiencing an incredible sensation of soaring silently above the valley with the river and forests far below your feet. You steer back towards Les Deux Alpes and land on the town slopes – for your best Bond impression, after a descent of 800 m (2624 ft). Paragliding is subject to weather conditions. Bookable through the ESF ski school (see page 75 for contact details).

SWIMMING POOLS & SPORTS CENTRE

Les Deux Alpes' open-air swimming pool

Les Deux Alpes has a 25 x 12 m open-air, heated, municipal swimming pool in the resort centre, next to the ice rink on rue des Sagnes (see town plans on pages 63 and 65). Free for holders of current Super Ski passes of at least six days' duration and for all children under 5 years of age; small admission charge otherwise. A whirlpool and sauna are also available at an extra charge. Bathing caps are obligatory, and are available on site. Open 14.30–19.00 hours +33 (0)4 76 79 22 73

Club Forme Health and Fitness Centre at the Grande Place in Les 2 Alpes 1800 has an indoor swimming pool, fitness suite, sauna, Turkish bath, whirlpool and squash courts. Swimming pool open 15.00–19.00 hours, closed Sat; other facilities open Sun–Fri 10.00–noon and 14.00–20.30 hours; Sat 14.00–20.00 hours +33 (0)4 76 79 25 64

SLEDGING

A dedicated sledging/toboggan slope is cordoned off at the base of the central town slopes next to the Lutins blue piste, close to the Jandri 1 gondola lift station (25). The slope is surrounded by inflatable crash tubes but is unsupervised. Free of charge for all responsible users but designated as a children's only facility.

VENOSC ARTISANS' VILLAGE

The tranquil village of Venosc is a commune of nine hamlets, terraced together on the sheltered wooded slopes of the Vénéon Valley. Here, local craftspeople have developed a charming artisans' village of craft boutiques in the quaint cobbled streets, an absolute contrast to the brash ski resort and offering a glimpse into the traditional l'Oisans soul.

The village is reached by the Venosc gondola lift (17); included on all ski passes and Pedestrian Passes, or available as a round trip by paying directly at the lift station. The upper station is located at the bottom of rue Sainte Luce in the Alpe de Venosc quarter of Les Deux Alpes (see town plan on page 65). The lift operates between 07.45–19.00 hours daily and takes 7½ minutes. On arrival, exit via the steps to the roadside, turn right and walk up the waymarked woodland trail by the stream to reach the village (5-minute walk uphill).

The Venosc Tourist Office is directly across the main road in front of the base station. It houses a small exhibition focused on local history and traditional life in the area, including a feature covering the region's once important slate-quarrying industry. Note that Monday is closing day for all Venosc's shops.

www.venosc.com

Venosc's artisans' village

APRÈS-SKI

Once the sun has set, the focus for fun turns away from the pistes and towards the attractions of the resort and the social side of the snowsports experience. Les Deux Alpes attracts a young and vibrant clientele and has plenty of diversions and facilities to appeal and cater to them. Those with an addiction to activity can still continue to ski on some evenings or try one of the extensive range of alternative activities and sports and leisure amenities available. The resort also has a fair-sized games arcade on the avenue de la Muzelle and two bowling alleys (see opposite). For later in the evening, there is a wide range of bars and restaurants and the town has a reputation for lively nightlife.

FULL MOON NIGHTS

Once per month, on the night of the full moon (dates vary every season, check before you visit), you can ski on the glacier until the sun sets, then enjoy a lively dinner with entertainment and dancing in Les Glaciers bar/restaurant at 3200 m (10,496 ft) before skiing back to resort by the light of the moon (or torchlight if necessary) for a vin chaud at the Slide Planet bar. A truly amazing experience and an unmissable event, unique to Les Deux Alpes. Must be booked in advance; price is inclusive of ski lifts, dinner, moonlit descent and reviving drink on return to resort. Bookings can be made through 2 Alpes Loisirs, whose office is in the place des 2 Alpes in the resort centre. ⓣ +33 (0)4 76 79 75 03

NIGHT SKIING & SLEDGING

From 20.30 to 22.30 hours on Tuesdays and Thursdays, the Lutins blue piste on the central town slopes is floodlit for night skiing. Access is included on all current ski passes.

BOWLING

An enduring favourite that is well catered for in the resort.

Bowling 'le Strike' Located at the rear of the place de Venosc in the Alpe de Venosc quarter. A large, full-size venue with a good choice of arcade games and a decent bar/café; two special lanes are set aside for children. Popular focal point for younger locals and normally buzzing in the evenings. Advance booking for bowling lanes recommended. Open daily 17.00–02.00 hours +33 (0)4 76 79 28 34

Bowling du Village Situated above the Grande Place in Les 2 Alpes 1800. Six bowling lanes (including a special children's lane), arcade machines, pool tables and a lively bar/café. Advance booking required for bowling lanes, particularly for late evening slots. Open daily 17.00–02.00 hours +33 (0)4 76 79 25 64

And the night begins... moonrise over Les Deux Alpes

PAMPERING

The trend for 'wellness' holidays in Alpine resorts continues to grow and the available facilities are improving all the time. Many of the larger 3- and 4-star quality hotels have their own in-house hydrotherapy suites, usually attached to fitness rooms; additionally, Les Deux Alpes also has two main spas to pamper and pummel:

Aquaflorès Spa Indoor and outdoor pool, sauna, Turkish bath, whirlpool, hydro massage, cardio-sculpt fitness suite, sports and relaxing massages, facials, body moisturizing and toning treatments, aromatherapy. ⓐ Based at the hotel Chalet Mounier, rue de la Chapelle ⓣ +33 (0)4 76 80 56 90 ⓦ www.chalet-mounier.com

Tanking Centre Flotation tanks, whirlpool, sauna, Turkish bath, fitness suite, sports massages and lymphatic drainage. ⓐ Galerie Lou Veno on avenue de la Muzelle ⓣ +33 (0)4 76 79 00 88

RETAIL THERAPY

Les Deux Alpes is a large conurbation with a year-round population and has around 120 retail establishments, although as with all ski resorts most of these are mountain sports equipment and clothing stores. All the main streets are lined with shops, but the upper avenue de la Muzelle in the Alpe de Venosc quarter has the largest range and most pleasant surroundings (see town plans on pages 63 and 65). Most shops stay open until 20.30 hours.

As well as the usual plethora of sports outlets, there are a fair number of boutiques, regional products delicatessens, patisseries and bakeries, souvenir shops and several large supermarkets; also a couple of pharmacies, perfumeries, specialist eyewear boutiques, newsagents, bookshops and photographic studios.

CAFÉS & RESTAURANTS

Les Deux Alpes has plenty of snack bars and cafés and more than 60 restaurants. A lot of the restaurants are quite average, with most offering similar bland international fare, but there are a number of more committed and noteworthy serious restaurants too. Most are open at lunchtime 12.00–14.00 hours, and in the evenings 19.00–23.30 hours. The following is a selection of some of the best (see town plans on pages 63 and 65).

Bel'Auberge €€+ High-quality, family-run gastronomic restaurant, tucked away down a quiet side street. Aspirational menu featuring seasonally influenced fish- and fine meat-based dishes. Perfect for a special occasion. 1 rue de la Chapelle, Alpe de Venosc quarter +33 (0)4 76 79 57 90

Le Rouge et Noir €+ Unpretentious and popular with locals; most noteworthy for staying open until 04.00 hours! Traditional regional specialities. rue de Grand-Plan +33 (0)4 76 79 02 51

Les Bleuets €+ Lively café/bar/restaurant popular with a younger crowd and with a slant towards snowboarding culture. Welcoming and friendly. Crêpes, pizzas and basic but wholesome home cooking, plus a range of cocktails. 2 rue de l'Irarde +33 (0)4 76 79 28 44

Le Cellier €€ Large, popular venue attractively decorated in the style of a rustic Alpine farmstead, focused around a huge, open wood-fire grill. Animated and buzzing ambiance. Specializes in regional specialities such as tartiflette, fondues and raclette (also vegetarian options). 3 place de Venosc +33 (0)4 76 79 08 79

L'Étable €€ Lovely, rustic traditional restaurant with a cosy and intimate atmosphere. Great range of salads, wood-fire oven pizzas and grilled meats. ⓐ 1 rue Saint-Claude, just opposite the Diable gondola station. ⓣ +33 (0)4 76 80 50 30

Crêperie de la Meije €+ Attractive café and salon de thé offering a wide range of crêpes. Homely and attractive. ⓐ 75 avenue de la Muzelle ⓣ +33 (0)4 76 80 52 10

Tribeca Caffé €€ Good Italian restaurant with a welcoming and animated ambiance, yet well away from the crowds. Wide range of pizzas, plus lasagne, pastas, etc. ⓐ 8 route de Champamé in the Alpe de Mont-de-Lans quarter ⓣ +33 (0)4 76 80 58 53

Les Sagnes €€ Pleasant café/restaurant in the style of an old stable. Small terrace with deckchairs. All-day café-bar service with crêperie/snacks available; chilled après-ski venue and more involved evening restaurant menu. ⓐ 90 avenue de la Muzelle (also accessible via rue des Sagnes) ⓣ +33 (0)4 76 79 51 62

BARS & CLUBS

Les Deux Alpes is renowned for being one of the liveliest ski resorts in the French Alps. It offers a wide choice of bars and two proper nightclubs, as well as plenty of quiet corners in which to pass the evenings. Venues are well spread out throughout the town, with concentrations around the central place des 2 Alpes, the Alpe de Venosc quarter and the Grand Place in Les 2 Alpes 1800. Most bars are open until around 02.00 hours, nightclubs until 04.00 hours. The following are some of the most popular (see town plans on pages 63 and 65).

Slide Planet An innovative feature of Les Deux Alpes' new-school 'Slide' ethos, based in the centre of the resort and combining a lively terrace bar, Internet café and games arcade with a retail outlet, rental shop and test station. Promoted as the après-ski social hub for the station's Snow Park and Slide zones and proving very popular as the place to chill with like-minded souls. Closes at 22.00 hours, except for special events. ⓐ 82 avenue de la Muzelle (just facing place des 2 Alpes) ⓦ www.slideplanet.com

La Grotte du Yéti Dutch/Danish tour operator-run in-house bar at their own chalet/hotel. Lively late-afternoon après-ski and frequent wild nights, with a good, varied programme of events, including live music and theme nights. ⓐ Place de Alpe de Venosc, on corner with rue des Vikings.

Le Pressoir Proper pub, with a relaxed and friendly atmosphere that attracts a good mix of ages and nationalities; retro, jazz and even country music! Good range of cocktails. ⓐ 73 avenue de la Muzelle in the resort centre.

Barrio Alto Small, hot basement music bar with a lively Latino ambiance: salsa, samba, merengue and bossa nova. Attracts a high percentage of French and Italian clientele. A fun and animated change from the more numerous Brit-centric venues. ⓐ Place de Venosc, in the Alpe de Venosc quarter.

Le Windsor One the resort's key pubs, with a friendly international bar team and a very lively atmosphere. Large terrace for early afternoon après-ski. Famous for its range of over 100 different beers and whiskys; wide range of cocktails too. ⓐ Avenue de la Muzelle.

The Lounge Cocktail lounge ambiance and faux classy decor, with deep red velvet curtains and intimate corners. Located right beside l'Avalanche nightclub. Perfect for pre-club warm-ups. ⓐ Rue du Cairou, in the Alpe de Venosc quarter.

O'Brians The name gives it away – it is an Irish bar, and a popular and lively one at that. Happy hours and frequent live music; disco-bar after 22.00 hours, with dancing encouraged. ⓐ Grande Place, Les 2 Alpes 1800.

L'Avalanche Les Deux Alpes' focal nightclub, going strong for over 15 years. International music policy with a Euro Dance and House bias. Promotional events and theme nights. ⓐ Rue du Cairou.

L'Opera Tucked away out of town, near the Grand Place at Les 2 Alpes 1800 – worth the effort of a taxi ride, though. Eclectic music policy and clientele. Located near a huge Club Med hotel and attracting its young and lively international crowd. Frequent live bands and themed events.

SPECIAL EVENTS

Les Deux Alpes organizes a varied programme of events and entertainment, including regular fireworks displays. Programme leaflets are printed on a weekly basis, distributed throughout the resort and available from the local tourist offices.

For details of all major ski competitions and festivals, please go to our website **www.ski-ride.com**

LA GRAVE
Vallons de la Meije ski domain

INTRODUCTION

Along with Chamonix and Mont Blanc, La Grave and La Meije are two of the most respected names in European mountaineering. To the Alpine cognoscenti La Grave and its Vallon de la Meije ski area are two of snowsports' most legendary destinations, redolent of the no-boundaries ethos of freeride and extreme skiing.

The primevally awesome peak of La Meije, which thrusts above La Grave village, was once believed to be unclimbable and was the last major peak in the Alps to be conquered. It is still regarded with awe. You can see why when you stand in La Grave and look up at the mountain's imposing sheer walls of gnarled rock, laden with ominous corniches and séracs.

Although access to the start of the ski routes is relatively straightforward, either using the two-stage cable car from La Grave or by linking in from Les Deux Alpes, over the deceptively easy pisted runs on the Glacier de la Girose, it should never be forgotten that once you begin your descent you have entered a serious mountaineering environment that can easily kill.

By now, you should be getting the idea that La Grave is no ordinary ski resort. In fact, it is not really a ski resort at all and definitely should not be regarded as such. It is a serious mountain station which just happens to facilitate snowsports as part of its remit to open up the high Alpine environment to all mountain and mountain-sports lovers.

PRONUNCIATION

La Grave La-grahve **La Meije** La-mej

Tackling the Vallons de la Meije

Other than three secured and pisted routes on the Glacier de la Girose, there are no pistes here. There are also no avalanche-protection systems, no slope signs and no boundary ropes; this is a mountain station in the true spirit of freeride. You can roam wherever your inspiration leads, but this requires a high level of technical ability and mountain expertise, ideally accompanied by a qualified local mountain guide (see opposite).

This philosophy is best encapsulated in La Grave's annual Derby de la Meije (first weekend of April), a free-for-all race from summit to base with no set route and no rules dictating which equipment you use – ski, snowboard, monoboard, blades, Telemark, Skwal, snowscoot, mountain bike (yes, you read that correctly), indeed anything except a paraglider. The first one to the bottom wins. Ⓦ www.derbydelameije.com

La Grave is a traditional, working mountain village in Isère's neighbouring Hautes-Alpes departement, straddling the N91 road between le Bourg-d'Oisans and Briançon. It has a handful of small hotels and bar/restaurants, a compact but well-stocked supermarket, a couple of regional products shops, a bakers and a launderette.

The base station for La Meije cable car is located just below the village, housing a ski pass sales kiosk and WCs, with some free car parking nearby. There is a ski-patrol hut by the lift station and every morning a patroller is on duty to answer questions on current routes' access, snow conditions and avalanche risk levels.

FURTHER INFORMATION

La Grave / La Meije tourist information office

Ⓣ + 33 (0)4 76 79 90 05 Ⓦ www.lagrave-lameije.com

BEFORE YOU SET OUT

The Vallons de la Meije domain is totally off-piste and is strictly for advanced riders/mountaineers only, preferably accompanied by a qualified mountain guide:

- Bureau des Guides ⓣ +33 (0)4 76 79 90 21 ⓦ www.guidelagrave.com
- Mountain rescue/ski patrol ⓣ +33 (0)4 92 22 22 22 ⓦ wap.la-grave.com

LA MEIJE CABLE CAR (1ER TRONÇON)

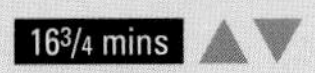

- 950 m (000 ft) vertical rise
- 360 passengers/hour
- 11¼ minutes from P1 mid-station

Strictly speaking this is a cable car installation, but it resembles a gondola lift: six trains of six-passenger cabins are hung in clusters of five and the lift operates on the pulse system, whereby the lift slows down at intervals on the journey to allow each cluster to pass through the stations. Waiting time between clusters is around 5 minutes. Halfway into the journey, you come to the big P1 lift pylon at 1800 m (5904 ft). A small platform here serves as a mid-point station, handy for avoiding the tricky lower sections.

This first section of the lift ascent arrives at Peyrou d'Amont at 2400 m (7872 ft). This is shared with the separate upper section of the cable car, housed in the front of the station on this same level. There are WCs here, and the cosy little Les Vallons bar/restaurant is immediately out to the left (see page 214). As with the P1 mid-station, this station can be reached from the slopes.

LA MEIJE CABLE CAR (2ÈME TRONÇON)

13¾ mins

- 800 m (000 ft) vertical rise
- 360 passengers/hour

The upper twin of the lower 1er Tronçon, providing the final uplift towards the glacial zone.

On arrival at the upper station at 3200 m (10,496 ft), simply walk straight out on to the compact Les Ruillans ridge ledge ahead left. There are WCs here and the Haut Dessus bar/ restaurant is directly ahead on this same level (see page 213). The off-piste descents start from this point: the classic Vallons de la Meije Route down the right-hand side of the lift line; the Chancel Route at the far side of the lift station. The pisted ridge track above left leads uphill to the Trifides button lift for the Glacier de la Girose and the link to Les Deux Alpes.

LES DEUX ALPES LINK

Not all ski passes permit access between La Grave and Les Deux Alpes; check with the ski pass office before setting out. To reach Les Deux Alpes, walk up the pisted ridge track ahead left from the upper La Meije cable car station and Haut Dessus restaurant to reach the Trifides button lift. Take that lift and go right to follow the waymarked glacier piste across to the Girose button lift towards the summit of the Dôme de la Lauze. From there, Les Deux Alpes' Lauze blue piste is about 10 minutes walk along a waymarked track via the wide ridge ahead right. On weekdays, a tracked vehicle provides a tow service (limited to 500 passengers per day).

CAUTION
Be aware that the link lifts close as early as 15.00 hours, and can close completely and unexpectedly if weather conditions deteriorate. If these lifts close, the only way back from Les Deux Alpes is an expensive 26 km/16¼ mile taxi ride.

TRIFIDES BUTTON LIFT

2¾ mins

- 100 m (328 ft) vertical rise
- 600 passengers/hour

The journey up hugs the rocky bulk of the Pointe Trifide, taking a dogleg around it at the mid-point. To the right is the Glacier de la Girose, with three pisted routes secured across it.

The scenery here is wild and imposing, with jagged aiguilles towering above and ahead. The serrated peak ahead right is Le Rateau at 3809 m (12,494 ft). The name means 'the rake', and it is so called because of its multi-pronged summit ridge.

On arrival, turn right; there are then two options. There is a blue-graded piste running down parallel to the lift line back to the get-on point, or you can follow the long, gentle marked traverse across the glacier towards the Girose button lift for the onward ascent and Les Deux Alpes link.

The design and engineering of the suspended lift cables serving these button lifts are unique in the world and are a real point of interest for technology buffs. The lift cables are looped through pulleys so that one continuous cable hauls both lifts, even though they run perpendicular to each other and some distance apart, requiring only one motor to power both lifts.

CAUTION

You are now on a glacier, where dangerous crevasses are numerous even if you cannot see them. The ski patrol have clearly marked out the secured routes and you are strongly advised to stay on them.

If you take off your skis or board, you become simply an unroped pedestrian in a serious mountaineering environment, so keep your gear on at all times when moving around on the glaciers.

GIROSE BUTTON LIFT

5½ mins

- 250 m (820 ft) vertical rise
- 600 passengers/hour

Since the glacier is in a constant state of flux, this lift's base 'pylon' is not fixed to the ground and instead is a counterweight suspended from the lift cables. This means that the get-on point can be moved to accommodate any changes in the ice flow. The lift operator's hut serves as an information point, with weather/avalanche risk and route conditions detailed on notice boards.

The upper section is quite steep. If you fall, stay within the roped lift-track area and carefully walk to the top. On arrival, dismount to either side. Ahead is the summit of the Dôme de la Lauze, with spectacular views towards the peaks of the Ecrins National Park and the starting point for the Vallée de la Selle off-piste route down to St. Christophe-en-Oisans. Turning ahead right takes you on to the summit ridge towards Les Deux Alpes ski area.

ROUTE DESCRIPTIONS

Please note that route descriptions for the classic Vallons de la Meije and Chancel routes are intended as general critiques and narrative to points of interest. They are not definitive route guides and are in no way a substitute for a qualified mountain guide.

CLASSIC VALLONS DE LA MEIJE ROUTE

The full descent of Les Vallons de la Meije has almost legendary status in the freeride snowsports world. It begins from Les Ruillans at 3200 m (10,496 ft), down the right-hand side of La Meije cable car line. The short drop-in to start from the ridge is steep and rocky, but not extreme. The top section is known as La Mure (the wall); it is steep, but not too demanding. The next section is wide and open and often gets tracked-out to an almost piste-like condition. You then have two choices: either to continue the descent veering down to the right, or to swing left to traverse on the contour line towards the cable car mid-station at Peyrou d'Amont at 2400 m (7872 ft).

Continuing the descent takes you down into the shadows of La Meije. Above to the right is overhung with huge séracs; major ice falls are a common occurrence here so keep moving and stay alert. You then come to a further split in the route: continuing straight down and veering left takes you into the tree line towards the P1 mid-station for the cable car; veering out to the right commits you to the full descent to the valley floor, requiring an advanced ability level to negotiate the next section. To finish, the run traverses along a narrow, steep ridge, wide to the lower right of the forest above a deep river gully, to the run-out to the small bridge across the Romanche River. Then hike up a steep path to reach the cable car base station and/or La Grave village.

CHANCEL ROUTE

The second classic route at La Grave, ranging out into steep and rugged terrain far to the left of La Meije cable car and accessing the incredibly extreme Banane, Terrace and Fréaux couloirs. There are two start points to the route: either across the crevasse-littered tongue of the Glacier de la Girose to the Col du Lac, or off the ridge at Les Ruillans from behind the Haut Dessus bar/restaurant and cable car station. Below the Col du Lac, both these upper sections then converge and the onward route descends through some steep and challenging rocky ground, with frequent drop-offs and little gullies, before traversing out to the left to reach the Refuge Chancel at 2508 m (8226 ft), arriving almost on the roof of the building. The Refuge Chancel is a fully functioning mountain refuge, with dormitories and a small bar/restaurant (see page 214). The refuge terrace offers a great vantage point to check out the extreme couloirs pouring off the rock face above the Lac de Puyvachier depression opposite.

The refuge is located above a cliff. To pass it you need to ride out wide to the left or right; when leaving the refuge itself, you need to ride out to the left. The next section down into the tree line gives a good workout over some wild and gnarly terrain, with a testing traverse through the forest to reach the P1 get-on point for La Meije cable car. Below this point, the tricky traverse continues through the forest towards a small bridge over a deep gully, with a nasty compression to the slope just before it flattens to run over the bridge. The lowest section is then relatively straightforward, joined from above right by the classic Vallons de la Meije route, for the final exit across a small bridge over the Romanche River. You then need to hike up a steep path to reach the cable car base station and/or La Grave village.

MOUNTAIN BARS & RESTAURANTS

Surprisingly, given the exclusively off-piste and wilderness approach adopted at La Grave, there are three good on-mountain bar/restaurants in the domain; this is France, after all, and food is important, particularly in this extreme environment. Two are based at the upper lift stations, and one is a proper mountain refuge out in the wilds of the Vallons de Chancel.

Haut Dessus €€

The most substantial of La Grave's three on-mountain venues, but still just a compact and really authentic wood-built mountain refuge.

Haut Dessus mountain bar/restaurant at 3200 m (10,496 ft)

A fair-sized terrace is furnished with plenty of bench tables and seating, with great views of the summit of La Meije and up and over the Glacier de la Girose to the peak of Le Rateau and the summit of the Dôme de la Lauze. A serving hatch to the terrace offers drinks and snacks, including wood-fired pizzas. Inside there is a small self-service restaurant, offering a basic selection of carbohydrate-loaded energy-rich fare, with a choice of simple salads and around three or four hot dishes, mostly pasta or meat/fowl with vegetables. The interior is bright and fairly cosy, with big windows overlooking the terrace towards the summits on the skyline beyond.

Les Vallons €+ Quaint and welcoming snack-bar/restaurant at Peyrou d'Amont at 2400 m (7872 ft). There is a small balcony terrace, just at the bottom of the lift station steps, at the end of the classic Vallons de la Meije upper route. The terrace has stunning views straight towards the north face of La Meije and the sérac fields hanging off its glacier.

Inside, there is a cosy bar with some tables and benches. The tiny dining area is upstairs and has a door leading directly into the lift station. A full bar service is offered, plus a basic but wholesome food menu including crêpes, mountain charcuterie and salads, regional sausages and chips, a good-value 'plat du jour' and home-made tarts and desserts.

Refuge Chancel €€ A proper, fully functioning rustic mountain refuge, with a dormitory available for overnight stays. The refuge also offers a basic bar and restaurant service, with meals focused on high-calorie energy-rich mountain fare such as tartiflette and lasagne with salads and chips.

A split-level terrace runs around the front and side of the building, giving absolutely breathtaking views over the Himalayan-scale scenery. This is a great vantage point for checking out the routes on the extreme Banane and Terrace couloirs above the nearby Lac de Puyvachier depression, as well as out over the Romanche Valley towards La Grave, the Aiguilles d'Arves and the Grandes Rousses. Inside, there is a plain but cosy dining room, with space by the entrance for leaving boots and hanging wet jackets. The refuge has a welcoming atmosphere, which is infused with a real *esprit de corps* among both visitors and the refuge guardians, all sharing a mutual respect for this stunning high Alpine environment. ⓣ +33 (0)4 76 79 92 32

OUT & ABOUT

Enjoying the region

OISANS & BEYOND

Although this book is a specialist guide to Les Deux Alpes and La Grave, and given that most readers will be visiting one of these stations specifically for a 1-week holiday, it would be a shame not to make a point of getting out of your resort for at least a morning to see more of this beautiful region. Having your own vehicle in resort opens up the whole of the Southern Alps, which are home to some major historical towns and cities (Vizille, Briançon and Grenoble) and important international ski stations (Chamrousse, Alpe d'Huez and the Grandes Rousses ski domain, Serre Chevalier and Mongenevre, the latter linked to the Milky Way ski domain in Italy). These are surrounded by a multitude of further satellite stations and smaller resorts (l'Alpe du Grand Serre, Puy-St-Vincent, Risoul and Les Orres), offering more than enough Alpine pistes, Nordic trails and ski lifts to ensure that you will not cross your own tracks again for weeks on end.

GRANDE GALAXIE

All Les Deux Alpes Super Ski passes of at least six days' duration permit a free-of-charge day pass to Puy-St-Vincent, Serre Chevalier/Briançon and the Milky Way (Via Lattea) stations, plus two days at Alpe d'Huez.

Alpe d'Huez is easily accessible by shuttle bus from Les Deux Alpes (see page 72 for details). You will need your own vehicle to reach the others.

ⓦ www.puysaintvincent.com	ⓣ +33 (0)4 92 23 35 80
ⓦ www.serre-chevalier.com	ⓣ +33 (0)4 92 24 98 98
ⓦ www.vialattea.it	ⓣ +39 (0)122 79 94 11
ⓦ www.alpedhuez.com	ⓣ +33 (0)4 76 11 44 44

LOCAL TRANSPORT

As well as the weekly shuttle between Les Deux Alpes and Alpe d'Huez (see page 72 for details), there are several buses daily from Les Deux Alpes to le Bourg-d'Oisans and Grenoble. From le Bourg-d'Oisans, there are also a number of buses daily to Grenoble via the Chateau de Vizille; plus free buses to the nearby villages of Allemont and Vaujany, the latter linked into the Grandes Rousses ski domain (Alpe d'Huez).

For further details, enquire at the local tourist offices in resort or contact the local transport company on avenue de la Muzelle: Agence VFD ⓣ +33 (0)4 76 80 31 60 ⓦ www.vfd.fr

LE BOURG-D'OISANS

The capital of l'Oisans, only 26 km (16¼ miles) from Les Deux Alpes. This is an attractive Alpine town with a good range of local shops and an interesting museum of Alpine minerals, crystals and fauna: Musée des minéraux et de la faune des Alpes (small admission charge) ⓣ +33 (0)4 76 80 27 54 ⓦ www.oisans.com/musee.bo

CHÂTEAU DE VIZILLE

The site of a historic regional assembly meeting (États du Dauphiné) on 21 July 1788. The assembly ratified a resolution that registered disapproval at King Louis XVI's meddling in politics and demanded recognition of individual freedom for all French citizens. The King reacted by banning all regional assemblies, helping to trigger the French Revolution. The Château de Vizille is thus seen as a cradle of the Revolution and houses France's only specialized museum dedicated to this period of French history. South-east of Grenoble, just 32 km (20 miles) from le Bourg-d'Oisans on the main N91 road. ⓦ www.musee-revolution-francaise.fr

LES DEUX ALPES IN SUMMER

It may never have occurred to you before to visit a ski resort in summer – after all what is there to do after the snow has melted? Quite a lot actually. The mountains are just as beautiful and even more accessible in summer, and the glaciers are still open for skiing throughout the high summer months. Away from the glaciers, many other ski lifts also reopen in summer to transport hikers, mountaineers and mountain bikers to the high ridges and peaks. The majority of the pistes may be green in colour now that the snow has gone, but the routes of the blue, red and black pistes still carry those gradings for downhill mountain biking. Pointing your wheels rather than your ski tips or board down the fall-line takes just as much skill and guts. White-water sports, quadbiking, bungy jumping and rock climbing are just some of the other ways in which summer visitors get their kicks. The après-jour in the resort bars and restaurants may be more mellow than the après-ski in winter, but there are still rocking venues if you know where to look.

Summer on the alpe

To escape from the stressful pace of modern life demands a more sophisticated alternative to the standard 'fly and flop' beach holiday. Why not try the natural active high of the mountains in summer?

SUMMER SPORTS & EVENTS

Splash-down at the Mondial du VTT

From mid June to the end of August, the Jandri Express cable cars carry snowsports enthusiasts up to the glaciers. The summer Snow Park on the Soreiller piste is one of Europe's biggest and hosts major summer freestyle competitions.

The station also hosts several major international mountain bike gatherings. The Mondial du VTT is a 4-day trade fair and equipment test event open to all, with a music and entertainment programme – including a mad splash-down competition where participants ride off a Big Air ramp to perform wild acrobatics into the resort's open-air swimming pool. Another major two-wheeled event is the spectacular Mountain of Hell race. From a massed start on the summit of the Dôme de la Lauze, competitors ride over the glacier and then all the way down to the finishing line at Les Deux Alpes.

Adrenaline junkies will also love the white-water rafting, kayaking and hydrospeed (white-water 'swimming' with a flotation device) available on the Vénéon River, easily accessible by the Venosc gondola lift. The most adventurous should also not miss the chance to experience one of the most incredible bungy jumps in Europe – 140 m (459 ft) from the Jandri 2 cable car!

Details of all summer activities and special events are advertised on the station's summer website, which is linked via **www.ski-ride.com** in the summer months.

GLOSSARY

Alpine skiing: the proper name for the sport of Downhill skiing, where participants use gravity to descend the slopes; as opposed to propelling themselves along.

Arête: a sharp ridge separating two glacial valleys or cirques.

Base station: the main access point and ski lifts departure point for a particular ski area; ideally the resort itself.

Base lodge: the main services building at the base station.

Bucket lift: a type of gondola lift where passengers stand in a basic open cabin, usually installed in hilly resort centres and lower slopes areas as public transport from one sector to another.

Button lift: a type of ski lift which consists of a pole hanging from the haul cable, fitted with a circular 'button' that is placed between your legs to pull you uphill.

Carver: a type of ski that is much wider at the tips (front) and tails (rear), allowing for wide, exaggerated turns on the piste.

Cirque: a semi-circular sweep of steep mountains surrounding a generally flat high-altitude valley; a product of glacial erosion.

Couloir: a steep and usually narrow gully sometimes called a chute.

Declutchable chair lift: the fastest type of chair lift, which disconnects from the fast haul cable at the passenger get-on and get-off points to allow for easier mount/dismount.

Drag lift: generic name for all ski lifts that pull passengers along whilst they are standing on the snow.

FIS: Fédération Internationale de Ski (International Ski Federation). The governing body of snowsports, which sets rules and regulations for piste safety and international competitions.

Freeride: a form of skiing away from the pistes where participants ride wherever and however the terrain (usually extreme) allows.

Funicular: a type of railway, usually steeply inclined.

Gondola lift: a type of ski lift where passengers ride inside a small cabin. Also called a Télécabine or Telecabina in Europe; smaller versions are also known as 'bubble lifts'.

Halfpipe: a specially prepared, semi-circular, pisted trough allowing users to ride up its high side walls to perform tricks.

Kickers: ramps of snow which provide a launch point for jumping high into the air.

Langlauf: the correct term for cross-country/Nordic-style skiing where skiers propel themselves in a walking or skating motion; Langlauf skis are much longer and narrower than Alpine skis.

Magic carpet: a conveyor belt.

Mogul (mogul field): bump (series of bumps) formed after heavy use of a ski slope has left the slope deeply rutted; advanced riders relish the challenge of riding through/over these bumps.

Monoskiing: a single large ski where binding attachments are side-by-side and close together.

Nordic skiing: see Langlauf

Nursery slope: a gentle slope designated as a beginners' area.

Off-piste: skiing/snowboarding away from the prepared ski slopes.

Piste: a way-marked slope/trail, where the snow has been groomed to make it easier to ski on. Pistes are graded by difficulty and colour coded to reflect this: green runs are the easiest; blue runs are slightly more challenging but still relatively easy; red runs are difficult slopes requiring technical ability from users; black pistes are the most difficult slopes reserved for expert users.

Piste basher: a tracked snowplough vehicle, fitted with a large rake with which to groom the pistes.

Rope tow: a basic ski lift consisting of a simple loop of rope, where users just grab on to be pulled along.

Schuss: the onomatopoeic term for skiing fast down a straight slope.

Ski school: the generic term for an organization which provides snowsports tuition.

Slalom: a form of skiing/snowboarding involving weaving in and out of a series of spaced poles/gates, normally against the clock.

Snow Park: a specially designated area set out with ramps (kickers), halfpipes and high rails for sliding along for performing tricks.

Snowshoe: a specialized form of footwear which spreads the wearer's weight over a greater surface area, making it easier to walk over snow.

T-Bar lift: a type of drag lift with a crossbar instead of a button, allowing two passengers to ride side by side.

Telemark skiing: an old form of classic Alpine skiing where the skier's foot is secured to the ski binding only at the toe end, requiring the skier to flex their ankle and knee to effect turns.

Tool point: a collection of spanners and screwdrivers, provided to allow experienced skiers/snow-boarders to adjust their own equipment.

EMERGENCIES

Emergency contact telephone numbers:

Piste security/assistance:	+33 (0)4 76 79 75 02
Medical emergencies	15
Fire	18
Police (Gendarmerie)	+33 (0)4 76 80 58 57
Hospital (Grenoble)	+33 (0)4 76 76 75 75

In the event of a serious accident:

1. Secure the area – plant skis in the form of an 'X' slightly above the position of any casualties, or have someone stand there to warn slope traffic; protect the victim from further injury.

2. First aid – ascertain the condition of the casualty and the extent of any injuries. Administer first aid only if you know what you are doing. Make sure the victim is kept warm and reassured.

A warm drink will help, but ONLY if the person has been fully conscious throughout; never give alcohol.

- If a limb appears to be fractured, protect it from further movement.
- If the casualty is unconscious, check to see that he or she is breathing; if not, start artificial respiration immediately.
- Place the casualty in the recovery position: gently roll the person on to his or her side, head down to prevent choking.

3. Alert the nearest station personnel and/or the piste patrol/emergency services. Make a note of the name/number of the nearest piste marker.

4. Exchange names and contact details with all parties to the accident, including witnesses and station personnel.

5. Get the casualty to shelter as soon as it is safe to move them.

PICTURE CREDITS

The publisher would like to thank the following for permission to reproduce their photographs: **Office du Tourisme de Les Deux Alpes** (J. P. Noisilier pp 1, 183, 194, 197, 218; Stéphane Cervos p 3; Juan Carmona pp 4, 95, 188; Bruno Longo pp 11, 61, 219; Paolo Biamonti p 215); **Comité Départemental du Tourisme de l'Isère** (E. Lecocq p 15); **Stephan Corporon** pp 12, 26, 33; **Sofia Barbas** pp 53, 77, 84, 118, 147, 160, 164, 192, 213. Original piste map artwork by **Vue d'ici**.